Police Con

In Yorkshire and Lincolnshire

(Part One)

By

James Marchbank

Copyright © 2021 James Marchbank

ISBN: 9798476968245

All rights reserved, including the right to reproduce this book, or portions thereof in any form. No part of this text may be reproduced, transmitted, downloaded, decompiled, reverse engineered, or stored, in any form or introduced into any information storage and retrieval system, in any form or by any means, whether electronic or mechanical without the express written permission of the author.

CHAPTER 1

ADVICE IN THE NIGHT

I was frightened, really frightened. I was on my way to command a firearms incident in a rural backwater. It was dark, stars were twinkling and the temperature outside was falling close to freezing.

I was a passenger in a car driven by a uniformed police sergeant who seemed to be enjoying the experience of hurtling round tight bends at excessive speeds and terrifying me at the same time.

The driver had been a friend for a lot of years. However, friendship brought no sense of safety. He collected cars like a spider collects flies, greedily and without much thought. The bulk of his growing fleet of vehicles were collected from Ebay, seldom serviced or maintained and disposed of as soon as their MOTs were due.

This particular vehicle was a Ford Probe and, from the outside, it looked quite a presentable vehicle. The inside, however, was a very different picture. The back seat was littered with cardboard pizza boxes, empty cans, rubbish filled carrier bags and other items of dubious origin in advanced stages of decay. As we screeched round bends on the narrow road the items rearranged themselves with the momentum. The only time we slowed down was when a Coca Cola can rolled under the cars control pedals and the driver took his foot off the accelerator to drag the can out.

I did not like commanding firearms incidents. Some of my colleagues loved it. They strutted around giving orders and being self-important. My view was that however well you managed the situation there was, by definition, someone armed with a lethal weapon whose purpose was to cause death, injury or mayhem. Those with the weapons were unpredictable and this alone rendered them dangerous.

After what seemed like an eternity, we entered a small village with a limited amount of street lighting. We passed a shop and a row of terraced housing and then came to a halt next to a pub, on the car park of which were a group of men one of whom was wearing the uniform of a police constable.

I beckoned the constable over to the car and asked what the situation was.

"The gunman is in that house over there, Sir. He's got his wife and kids with him, at least they say he has," said the constable indicating the group of men as being his source of information.

One of the men walked over to our vehicle,

"He's a right daft bastard is yon," he said. "He's always pulling stunts like this!"

After a brief discussion I ascertained that the gunman lived in the cottage across the road. He had been seen to drag his wife and children out of his car and into the house. While doing this he was carrying what looked like a rifle or a shotgun. This fitted with the information I had been given before setting off to the village. The wife had taken the children to her parents in a neighbouring village for tea. Husband had turned up demanding his wife returned with him and when she declined, he produced a shotgun. The parents had reported the incident to the Police.

The message that is drummed into every Police Firearms Commander during training is that from this point on you should seek to isolate and contain the armed person or persons. Well, the good news in this case was that the gunman had contained himself. The bad news was that he had potential hostages with him.

From this point on if anything went wrong it would be viewed as my fault. Any decisions I made would be analysed and dissected by people who were probably in bed as I was making those decisions. No one was speaking, all eyes seemed to be on me. The sergeant, the constable and the onlookers were all waiting to be told what to do and, in an attempt, not to disappoint I asked the crowd to move as far away as possible. Sullenly the men strolled a little further from the cottage and the pub.

At this point, to my relief, a marked Police Transit Van drove into the village and pulled on to the pub carpark. I walked over to it and was pleased to see the first officer who disembarked. He was a Firearms Tactical Advisor; that is someone whose day job involves training with Firearms Officers, planning tactics and maintaining weapons. He knew the capabilities of his team and, probably, the best strategy to adopt far better than I did.

He had a broad grin on his face as he approached me.

"Have you got your handcuffs on?" He asked.

This was a reference to an earlier occasion which had caused me a considerable degree of embarrassment. I had attended a Firearms Commanders Training Day which was held in a disused quarry not far from the Police Station at which I was based. The event involved a group of colleagues and myself watching a Firearms Team going through its paces. The idea was to familiarize us with the capabilities of the teams, a nice quiet day of watching others do the work with a free lunch thrown in. As usual there was no such thing as a free lunch. We were told that we would be playing the role of hostages who would be rescued by Firearms Officers

We were handcuffed and led into a building constructed of breeze blocks and with no lighting. We were seated on a row of chairs and left there. There was no need for blindfolds as it was pitch black inside the building. There was none of the usual chit chat among my colleagues and the silence seemed to add to the tension.

After what seemed like an age, we heard a loud bang followed by distant shouting then a second bang and finally bright lights were being shone on us. More alarmingly the red dots of infra-red sights moved across us and round the room. We were eventually dragged blinking out of the building and into the day light.

I am sure I was not alone in feeling disorientated and there was little by way of aftercare from our 'rescuers'. Indeed, as my colleagues were freed from their handcuffs one by one, I sensed that something was not quite right. No one was looking at me or seeking me out for release!

My apprehension was fully justified. The tactical advisor, now with me at the current incident, came over and informed me that the officer who had handcuffed me could not find his key. Various other keys were tried and there was a degree of twisting, straining and pulling, none of which resulted in my being released.

An officer was dispatched to try and find a duplicate key and I remained with my hands behind my back, standing in a muddy quarry as the first spots of rain began to descend. This was still the situation when several minutes later it was decided that we had to go for the lunch which had been booked at a local pub.

Now a situation that I thought was bad was about to become even more embarrassing. The quarry, as I have said, was located near to the police station I worked at. At this time, I was the Divisional Commander of the area, in charge of some two hundred police officers and fifty civilian staff. One of my responsibilities was managing the police response to licensing issues and deciding whether or not we would oppose the grant of liquor licenses. I had recently had a hostile response when addressing the Licensed Victuallers Association at their annual dinner. I was about to enter the premises of a licensee wearing full uniform and handcuffs!

To be fair to the Landlord he did not make too much of the situation, though I did see him smiling as a constable tried to feed me steak pie and chips on a spoon. Fortunately, I did not need to visit the toilet and by the time the pudding arrived so did the key. Freedom had seldom felt so sweet.

Greetings and subconscious reminiscences out of the way we set about planning how we would deal with the gunman. The firearms team covered the corners of the building while the arrival of two police dog handlers meant that German Shepherds would be an option if the armed man attempted to run from the cottage. Traffic had been diverted away from the street where we were located and things started to take on a more controlled feel.

I remained on the Pub Car Park awaiting the arrival of a Force Negotiator. Such individuals were trained in how to communicate with people who placed themselves in positions which threatened their own or others' lives. It had been decided that the Negotiator in this case would ring the gunman from a landline telephone in the pub. This was considered a good idea as the Force Helicopter was about to arrive and radio and mobile communication could be compromised.

The sergeant, who only half an hour earlier had been hurtling us towards our current location, brought me a cup of tea. As he did so the Helicopter thudded onto the scene and hovered some thirty meters above our position. The downdraft made trees and shrubs sway violently. The cottage was illuminated by the machine's huge spotlight.

"Is that one of them Heliflipcopters?" a voice asked me.

I turned to see an old man with white hair wearing a checked shirt and jeans. He was only two or three feet from me and mysteriously everyone else had disappeared from the car park.

"Will it tummel down on us?" he asked, looking genuinely concerned.

I assured him that the Helicopter and crew were most unlikely to fall down on us and suggested that he go back to his house till things quietened down.

"What's he done now then?" asked the man. "He's alus pulling some stunt or other, is he pissed up again?"

This was interesting. We had confirmed that the man had dragged his wife from his parent in laws but we had no motive for his action. No one had mentioned alcohol before and clearly this could have an impact on both his behaviour and the course of the negotiation.

"Have you any reason to believe that the man from the cottage has been drinking today?" I asked.

"Well, it had to be a bloody unusual day if he hadn't been at it, he likes his lotion. I reckon the pub would go bust if you shot him. Are you going to shot him?"

I explained that the idea was to talk him into coming out peacefully and that if he attempted to run from the cottage, we had police dogs ready to catch him.

"I had a dog once," my new friend offered before continuing, "I had a wife too." There was a pause and then he said, almost as an afterthought, "I miss the dog."

There was no mention of whether or not he missed his wife.

The Negotiator arrived and after we had a brief chat, he walked over to the pub in order to ring the gunman.

"If you'd asked, I'd have gone and got him to come out". My companion offered.

I did not reply. Indeed, I was getting a bit irritated with his failure to go away.

"Thirty coppers, dogs, a Heliflipcopter and four vans. Where are you when there's real work to be done. There's no wonder folks has no confidence in you. The bloke has got pissed, got hungry and gone and got his wife to make his tea. It's simple and if you'd asked, I'd have got him out."

The old man made it sound so simple, yet all my experience suggested that it was not. I again suggested that he go back to his house for his own safety, but I had no spare officer to physically escort him. And I just knew that there would be more home spun wisdom to come. I was not wrong!

"You see you've lost the respect of the public. No one's frightened of you. You're too nice. Him over there, he'd have never done this if he was scared of you. You need to top a few. Quick lime's the answer. Get a few of them speeders, take them somewhere quiet, finish them off and cover them in quicklime. When word got round there'd be no speeders and no need for all these coppers with guns just 'cos a bloke's hungry"

Some twenty minutes later the gunman left the house with his hands on his head. He was told to lay down, which he did immediately and he was then approached by armed officers who handcuffed him, exactly as they had done to me on the earlier occasion. The gun was recovered and was found to be an unloaded single barrelled shotgun.

The negotiator walked towards me across the car park, gravel crunching under his feet. For the first time I realized how cold it had become and I envied the fact he had spent the last hour in the relative warmth of the pub.

"Well, that's another one sorted."

"Why did he do it?" I asked.

"Apparently he had been drinking in the pub and got hungry. He was upset that his wife was not at home to cook his supper, so he went to get her...." The negotiator seemed ready to tell me more, but my companion interjected.

"I told you that's what it was all about. Sumut and nowt like it alus is."

"Have you got any more advice for me before we leave, I asked?"

He looked at me strangely, his brow furrowed as if he was deep in thought and he said,

"Never marry a ballet dancer."

"Why?" I asked, genuinely intrigued.

"Well, they'll alus be bloody knackered won't they. All that training and dancing. They'll be fit for nowt when they come home. No cooking, no cleaning, no nowt. All show and uselessness."

"Was your wife a ballet dancer?" I asked, hoping to sound sarcastic.

"No," he admitted and then, "she worked at Tesco, didn't she?"

He then wandered off into the night. It had been a surreal encounter. I felt like I had been watching myself from somewhere out of my body. Events were taking place and I did not feel in total control of them. It was a feeling that I had had several times during my police career.

I never saw the old man again and never found out what they called him. He had been correct about what had caused the incident. I also followed his advice and never married a ballet dancer, my wife also worked for Tesco, at least she did for a short time. Would his advice about speeders have been good.... I never got the chance to find out.

One thing was certain, however, the old man was one of the myriads of characters that I met in a thirty-year police career and at the end of the day characters are what made that career worthwhile and created the lasting memories. The characters are the reason for my attempts to write about my career.

CHAPTER TWO

BEGINNINGS

I drifted into joining the Police Service. There was no master plan, no grand design or burning vocation to help and protect the public. I had been to university, worked as an articled clerk for a firm of solicitors, trained for management with F.W.Woolworths and finally, uncertain what to do next, I had joined the Police.

I have tried to explain this lack of a career plan to many people over the years and very few of them have believed me. The facts do not seem to support it. My fathers' uncle was an inspector in the Leeds City Mounted Police. Whenever I asked about him, I was told that he could throw a horse down with one hand and he had always wanted to adopt me. Both these assertions raised more questions than they answered. Why would anyone want to throw a horse down, with one hand or two? More significantly, for me, why would he need to adopt me when I had two living and loving parents?

My aunties second husband was a constable in the West Riding Constabulary and his son, by an earlier marriage, also joined and became a detective in that Force.

For many though, the most compelling piece of evidence of my predestined career path was that my father was a Police Officer. He spent thirty years policing the streets of Keighley and Bradford, patrolling the fringes of the Yorkshire Dales in a Police Traffic Car and finally working as the Force Road Safety Officer.

However, these superficial facts conceal the real truth.

My father had been born in Leeds not long after the 'Great Strike'. He became an apprentice engineer with Crabtree's Engineering and did well. I am told he won awards for his skilled work and, but for Mr Hitler, his life could have been very different. Crabtree's was bombed flat and after the war he was offered a job engineering in South Africa. By then he had met my mother who did not want to leave England.

To pursue his romance the city boy would motorcycle from Leeds into the Dales where my mothers' family lived. He spent the week ends potholing and playing rugby for North Ribblesdale but could find no work in the area where he wanted to be. The Police seemed the only way to get a job where he could be near my mother and get paid at the same time. This master plan was to backfire, but the dye was cast.

My father started work as a police officer in Settle, not far from Langcliffe where my mother had been born in the village shop run by my grandfather. It seemed that the future was bright, but police regulations were soon to take a hand in events.

In those days a police officer was not allowed to live in the same place that their spouse came from. Thus, as soon as my mother and father were married, they had to uproot and move to a different area. Keighley was certainly different from Settle!

I remember Keighley from being about five years old. Those memories are mainly of an industrial town with fine old buildings, huge mills and factories, but the lasting impression was that everything was black. The buildings, industrial or not, were caked in generations of smoke from coal fires. The town centre was a drab, crowded place built around a bus station.

I came to love Keighley, particularly Cliffe Castle which was a large house donated to the town by Sir Bracewell Smith, a Keighley boy and former Lord Mayor of London. I also liked the fact that whenever you looked up you could see hills without buildings on them. But if I came to love the town my mother never did, she was a fish out of water.

The first house we lived in was on Spencer Street, a terraced, back-to-back construction, built with hundreds of others to house the mill workers of the town. It had an outside toilet, ice formed on the inside of the windows in winter and you had to walk up a steep hill to get to it. Most memorable for me was the fact that the Spencer Street house had silver fish. As a small boy it seemed quite exotic to have fish living in the house but the reality was very different. Silver fish are a small insect like creature that shine when light reflects on them and which squirm and move very quickly. They are usually found in houses that are afflicted with damp. Spencer Street must have been very damp because they got everywhere, they were found between slices of bread, in books, under the rugs, literally everywhere.

We moved from Spencer Street to Parkwood Street when I was six years old. The new house, was a semi-detached, recently built property with a large garden. My recollections of Parkwood Street are of a fairly good place to live, with a nearby wood to play in and much more space than Spencer Street. I cannot recall people shouting things about "Coppers" as they walked past, though my mother can and she disliked the new house as much as the old one.

Two events were about to happen that would really challenge the theory that I was destined for a career in the Police Service. Both events were a direct result of the application of Police Regulations of Service, that very set of rules that moved my family to Keighley in the first place.

The house that we lived in on Parkwood Street was a Police House, that is, it was owned by the Police Force in the same way that it owned Police Stations and Police cars etc. The house was an asset and, therefore, regulations required that assets should be looked after. Every piece of police equipment was inventoried down to the number of staplers in a particular office. Houses were treated exactly the same and they had to be inspected and inventoried at set intervals.

Now in those days police officers were required to parade when they came on duty and be checked to ensure their uniforms and equipment were smart and cared for. It was expected that shoes or boots would be highly polished, trousers pressed, torches working and nothing missing from what had been issued. It was very militaristic and the same principles were applied to inspecting houses.

A sergeant or an inspector would arrive at the house in full uniform with a clipboard and papers. We were required to leave the house and stand outside. The inspector then walked past us and began his inspection. Every room and their contents were checked and it was not unusual for drawers and cupboards to be opened. In later years when I was the victim of a series of burglaries, I felt violated because someone had been through my private belongings. It was a very similar experience having a police house inspection. Some of the things inspected did not even seem relevant to the state of the police house, for example "Contents of Pantry."

When the inspection was over the inspecting officer merely stated that a report would be submitted. This indeed did happen and probably made its way onto the desks of several senior officers before my father was eventually told if the house had been declared satisfactory. To me the whole process was humiliating and unnecessary, but at least it happened to everyone. This was not the case with the second event.

My mother had for a short period of time attended an Agricultural College in Monmouth. She did not complete the course as her mother died and she returned home to help look after her family. All that she took home with her was a lifetime interest in farming. This interest was revived when she inherited a small amount of money on the later death of her father. After a discussion with my father, she decided she would rent a smallholding and buy a small number of beef calves to fatten for sale.

This indeed happened and my brother and I quickly gave the calves names and they became honorary family members. There was Tarzan, Samson, Bluey and four or five others who shared a large hillside field with several chickens and one sheep. For a short period, it was a fantastic experience, feeding, cleaning and just generally being around the animals. Then someone in the police community reported my father for having a business interest incompatible with his role as a police officer.

In those days it did not matter that the business interest was that of the officer's spouse, nor could anyone explain how keeping cattle was incompatible with being an impartial police officer in an industrial town. The cattle had to go or my father had to resign, he had a month to state which it would be. There was really only one choice and the cattle departed at a loss; without the cattle the rented field was pointless and the advance on that was also a loss. We later found out that the business interest had been reported to senior police management by one of our neighbours.

So, all in all the Police were not my favourite organization and there were other incidents over the years that reinforced these early impressions. After a charity fund raising event, when I was at university, two plain clothes police officers pushed me up against a wall to search me "because you've got long hair and look suspicious". They then tipped out five hundred old penny pieces that I had raised from Roll a Penny at the fund raiser, "because we need to look in the bag". After ten minutes bent down picking them all up again off a wet pavement, I was ready to be quite anti police.

However, in the interests of balance I must say that being a policeman's son was not all bad. As a small boy I remember the Christmas parties with a lot of warmth. Somebody, or group of bodies, really made a special effort. Harry H. Corbett and Sooty came at least twice and Mr Pastry, who was rather more than just a clown, was a particular favourite of mine. We also got a paper carrier bag with an apple and orange inside, a book and one larger Christmas present. It was all simple, unsophisticated stuff like musical chairs, blind man's bluff and the like but it must have been great fun or I would have forgotten it.

I also enjoyed going with my father round the local agricultural shows. The Police Force had a huge tent which was only slightly smaller than those used as the Big Top at a circus. It was used to display road safety information, vehicles that had been in crashes and film shows giving advice to road users. In later years there was even a driving simulator where you sat in a mock car with a steering wheel, accelerator and brake, then 'drove' as a film was shown on a screen in front of the 'vehicle'. I only had one go and got an electric shock off the accelerator pedal, nowadays I could have made a claim for compensation but it was a different world then.

My father used to collect all the gear for the shows from Police Headquarters. It was transported in a large van of the type used to move furniture from one house to another. The van was quite old and it had a shiny steel Indian Chiefs' head on the bonnet. I was not allowed to be carried in the van as only police personnel were insured. On one occasion I had cause to be grateful that I was not allowed to travel in it.

My father picked up the van as usual and it had already been loaded. A piece of boarding protruded from the storage area of the van into the driver's cab. From the driver's seat it was impossible to see either the passenger or anything on the vans nearside. A police cadet sat in the passenger's seat and a second cadet was in the rear of the van. As they drove along and reached junctions my father would ask the passenger in the front if they were alright to the left. When an affirmative reply was received, they moved across the junction and towards their destination.

After traveling some way, the question was asked again, "Alright, left?"

"Yes" came back the reply and my father eased the van onto the junction. Seconds later there was a shuddering bang to the left side of the van. Investigation revealed that an ice cream van had driven into the police removal van. Neither vehicle was too badly damaged but the result of the collision was obvious to see. My father was more than a little cross.

"I thought I asked you if it was alright" He asked angrily.

"I thought you were asking if I was alright!" blurted the tearful cadet.

They had driven miles, crossing several junctions, with a total lack of communication between driver and passenger. It was incredible there had not been a collision sooner.

Now, up to this point I have presented a few reasons why it was unlikely I would be attracted to the Police Service. However, when I have outlined these arguments to friends over the years, they have still not been convinced that my joining up was not predestined.

"Ah!" They say, "You will have seen your dad doing things and heard him talking about it and the whole lot will have soaked into your subconscious."

So, I guess the question is what do I remember my father doing or talking about in relation to policing? Sadly, the answer is that I remember very little of what he said at first hand. My mother, who is still alive, tells me that he turned down a number of promotion opportunities so that the family did not have to move house while my brother and I were at school. She says that he disliked many of his peers, believing them to be "back stabbers" and sycophants willing to climb over each other for their own advancement. I do not remember him saying these things, my memories are of a different nature.

He told me once that he was patrolling a Dales Village on a Sunday. He was still very young in service and he was enjoying being paid for walking in the countryside. Years before my father found himself charged with looking after the village there had been a murder at the local pub. As a result, all licensed premises in the village were closed. This was, however, a working community and Sunday was the only day of rest. A local entrepreneur had taken to serving beer in jam jars from a barrel that he kept in his outside toilet. The drinkers huddled down a narrow passageway smoking and drinking their illicit alcohol and it was there that my father found them on this particular Sunday morning.

This would have been a difficult and complicated matter for a lone rookie constable to have dealt with and I suppose my father was more pragmatic than zealous. They handed him a jam jar of the local brew and he took his helmet off. Things might have run a pleasant convivial course but at that moment the local police sergeant walked onto the village green. My father put the jam jar into his jacket and went to meet the sergeant.

Together they set off to walk round the village. My father was acutely aware of the smell of the beer as it slopped out of the jar and down into his underpants. The sergeant did not seem to notice and they continued to cross a river on stepping stones, climbed a wall and scaled a woodland bank. They walked for well over an hour until my father's shift of work was nearly over. At this point the man with the stripes drew himself up to his full height and said,

"Now then Lad. Lest you think I'm as daft as you obviously are. Get rid of that jam jar down your pants and if I ever catch you drinking on duty again your feet will not touch".

My father escaped with his job but went home to his lodgings with a wet crutch and smelling like a barmaid's apron. The sergeant had known all along what had been happening. Lesson? You are never as clever as you think you are.

The other story I remember him telling was also from his years working in the Dales though by this time he was driving a Jowitt Javelin Police Traffic car. The adventure he recounted resulted in the local newspaper carrying the following headline, "Police heroes capture escaped Lion." The reality was less dramatic.

A lion had in fact escaped from a circus in the nearby town. It had been seen making its way up into the hills and fears were directed more towards what it might do to grazing sheep than any threat to local residents. For several days there had been no sign of the lion nor any reports of sheep having been killed.

My father and his companion were driving along a narrow road high in the hills. They were looking for somewhere to have their sandwiches. As they slowed down to negotiate a cattle grid something moved along the wall nearby. It was the lion.

The two officers looked at each other, no doubt both hoping that their companion would have a flash of inspiration. Eventually they decided that they had to do something. Nowadays an officer would contact Headquarters and assistance would arrive like the Seventh Cavalry riding over the hill. There would be Firearms Teams, vets, Dog Handlers and their canine friends and a whole host of others. Then, with a radio that only worked sporadically, the officers on the scene could either drive to find a telephone or do something themselves.

The Traffic Car had a rope in the boot and the two 'heroes' decided that they were going to capture the lion! This plan was more sneaky than bold. The lion had huddled itself against the wall, making no attempt to run away from the noisy car. The officers made a noose at the end of the rope and then drove across the cattle grid and up the other side of the wall on the grass. The passenger got out of the car walked about two feet and lowered the noose over the wall. As planned the noose went over the lion's head and mane and the capture was completed with a quick tug. The passenger then got back in the car. My father reversed onto the road and back over the cattle grid. The slack in the rope was pulled in until the lion was being dragged away from the wall. The King of the Jungle raised itself arthritically and stumbled towards the car which my father drove off as slowly as possible.

Over an hour later the car, the officers and a very tired lion arrived back at the circus it had escaped from. It never roared once and went back in its cage without any prodding or pushing. In reality it was exhausted after three days in the hills with no food. It was also almost toothless and slightly lame...but that was left out of the news story!

I know this story was true and that is more than can be said about some of my father's non police stories. He was a great story teller and he used to entertain my brother and I to tales of his times as a wrestler who fought under the name of 'The Iron Duke'. There were also potholing stories, such as the time that he was trapped underground and existed by eating the miraculously preserved flesh of a baby mammoth and of the German spy who, having parachuted onto the moors, walled himself in a cave where he died.

However, the fact that such a wonderful story teller never spoke much about his Police career reinforces my belief that I was not exposed to any subconscious "Join the Police" messages.

Years later I attended the Police Staff College, more of which later, and met a man called Rob Adlam. He lectured on the subject of whether or not there was a Police Personality. That is, did a certain psychological profile cause people to be drawn to a career in Policing. Basically, tests were conducted to find out what character traits an individual had. Were they, for example, introvert or extrovert? If the results showed the subject to be Extrovert, Sensing, Thinking and Judging there was a strong possibility they would be attracted to the Police Service. This theory had one weakness, as the individuals tested were already Police Officers, there was also the possibility that they had learned how to portray the traits that they found made them acceptable once in the organization. I may have got this slightly wrong but my results did not fit anyway.... more evidence that I should have been a Stage Actor and something had gone wrong!

CHAPTER THREE

IF NOT DESTINY

When I started at Keighley Boys Grammar School it was housed in an old Victorian building in the centre of the town. By modern standards it had few facilities, everything was old, there were no playing fields just a large tarmacked yard. It was, however, a school with good academic success records, the masters wore gowns, the sixth form had stripey blazers, it was steeped in tradition.

A year after I arrived it burned down. I had nothing to do with it but like most of the town I was there when the roof collapsed into the flames. After a time, the school was relocated to a greenfield site where the name was changed to Oakbank Grammar School and then, after the arrival of girls, to Oakbank School.

After the first year I enjoyed school, though I cannot claim to have been an academic high achiever. I ran for the school cross country team, played a bit of rugby and competed at athletics with Bingley Harriers. In my last years as a schoolboy, I started to work during the summer holidays and this continued when I went to university. I worked for the Airedale Cornish Pasty factory making puff pastry in industrial quantities, putting the eggs into the centre of Gala Pork Pies and loading delivery trays. I also worked for Skipton Council one year, helping a dry-stone Waller up on the hills.

I remember being called to see the geography master one day and as usual worried that I had done something wrong or forgotten to even do the something. He quickly explained that he was now the school Careers Master and he wanted to know what I wanted to do when I left school. My first reaction was that I did not want to leave, it was a reality I had not considered! After a time, I told him I'd like to study History, my favourite subject, at university.

"What will you do with that?" He asked, looking at me as if I had said something extraordinary.

"All you could do is end up a teacher like me. You don't want that do you.?"

I cannot remember replying to any of this and eventually he gave me a pamphlet issued by the Law Society spelling out how lucrative a career as a Solicitor could be.

A year later I started studying Law at Hull University. I could have gone to Liverpool but I thought it was a dirty dump and the man who interviewed me was, I thought, rude and arrogant. When I went to Hull the cherry trees were in bloom, it was a sunny day and the people were welcoming. Superficial things have always seemed to have an inordinate impact on me!

The Law and I were not a well-matched combination. I hated it, from the first day I wanted to change subjects. It wasn't that I couldn't understand the concepts it ran much deeper than that! I had had a fairly sheltered childhood, I did not know what a mortgage was, no idea why anyone would want to get divorced and I had studied Biology instead of Latin. The course seemed to dwell on the Law relating to things like Trusts but it never explained what a trust was. I tried learning things by heart but it was soul destroying. How I got my degree is a mystery to me and I am equally sure it was a surprise to my tutors.

I was not certain I wanted to be a lawyer and when I saw a poster advertising a scholarship in the United States it seemed a good way of delaying a career decision. The application form was only a page long and did not seem to ask any really pertinent questions about why you wanted a scholarship. The gist was that there was a course designed to look at "Environmental Issues and Mans' role in the World". If successful you got free flights to and from America, free food and lodging and several days sponsored sightseeing.

The interview was, to my surprise, conducted in a terraced house in a run-down area of Hull. The interview room was clearly a kitchen when in normal usage and it smelled of a cross between bacon and patchouli oil. Those conducting the interview did not seem to fit the surroundings, they were smart and distinguished looking. The main man was, I think, called

Douglas Orme and he carried an aura of authority I later found in some Police Chief Officers.

The only thing I remember being asked was whether I would give up the Law if an alternative career opportunity arose? This was easy, I would probably give it up if there was no other career opportunity.

Three weeks later I flew to New York with some thirty other students from around the United Kingdom. It was my first flight and I thoroughly enjoyed it. The food was good, the seats comfortable and seeing ice bergs from thirty thousand feet was quite exciting. No one seemed to have much idea about what we were going to be doing but I was pretty certain it would be better than studying Trusts!

Doubts started to creep in when we left John Kennedy airport. We were greeted by a large group of Asian men who threw things at our bus. The men were Koreans and they were throwing rose petals, no one had ever done that to me before and I think the experience was new to most on the bus!

We were driven into the suburbs of New York to a place near Tarrytown and halted at one end of a long, very tall wall. An electric gate slid open and we entered the grounds of an impressive house. The bus travelled almost a mile and stopped in front of the house where we were invited to disembark and collect our suitcases.

Within minutes we had been shown to a dormitory filled with bunk beds and lockers and herded back downstairs to where the bus had brought us. Everyone was given an apple and told that we would each be designated a friend and guide who would help us during our stay. These friends then arrived, almost like a magic trick, and issued us with a name tag. My friend was called Tom.

Tom suggested that we went for a walk round the grounds and we set off to do this, some twenty meters behind another pair and with a further couple behind us. As we walked, we talked about football and England and the differences between there and America, then Tom introduced the Unification Church into our conversation. He was a member of the Church and had been with them for some years, he had found himself as a follower of the faith and had willingly surrendered all his goods to the Church. His day job was selling candles and books for the Church funds.

It was the funds that Tom and his fellow believers raised that had paid for the current group of students to travel to America. I was a guest of the Unification Church who were led by Sun Myung Moon. It was hoped that many of us would relinquish the material world and remain with the Church family when our three weeks were up. We were the guests of an organization which briefly became notorious in the UK. An organization that became known as the "Moonies"

I think it is fair to say that all of us 'scholarship' winners were in a state of shock when we went to bed that night. The following morning things got worse. After being woken early and allowed to wash we were taken to various parts of the grounds and allowed to pray before being marched back to the house. After a few minutes standing and wondering what would happen next a couple of Church members with guitars joined us. They began to sing the American National Anthem and various other patriotic songs to which we were encouraged to sing along. This was followed by the issue of an apple to everyone and a request to surrender any money for safe keeping.

Now the Moonies might have had the upper hand and the benefit of shock tactics but they were not having my money. I put a little in the envelope they provided us with but kept the bulk of what I had in my back pocket. As we were led to our first lecture several other students were claiming to have similarly secreted their cash, I was not alone and it was not just a Yorkshire thing!

The first lecture, conducted in the grounds, was entitled simply "Anti Communist Input". The rest of the day was to involve study of the Divine Principles on which the Unification Church was based. Each morning we were woken early and taken to think about the Divine Principle in a secluded spot, we were then given an apple and lectures began again. I do not know when or if the Church Members slept as they were up when we awoke and still praying when we went to bed. Looking back, I would say that the whole set up was geared to producing a brain washing effect. We wandered around like zombies and events just flowed over us.

It was not all bad, we were taken to see the Empire State Building and, on the way, back we found ourselves at the West Point Military Academy talking to Cadets in Training. However, for me claustrophobia began to set in. We had not seen a newspaper, the television or heard the radio since we arrived. Most of us had not managed to contact our parents by phone and there was a rumour that cards and letters we submitted were still in a tray in the Church Office.

Eventually I found a kindred spirit who, like me, still had some money. We decided to wait till lights out then get out of the grounds and see if we could find the nearest town with a phone and a bar. The Great Escape was achieved by climbing out of the bathroom window and over the perimeter wall using a ladder we found at the side of the building.

Our first mission was a fantastic success. We found a bar and after a beer or two we explained to the Barman what was happening to us. He was sympathetic and generous giving us a lift back to the Church when closing time came. We got back in without discovery and dozed our way through the following days Divine Principle input.

The same escape route was used on a couple of other occasions but it was too good to last and one night we could not get back in. We went to the gate and were eventually collected by Church officials.

Not to put too fine a point on it we were asked to leave. It was clear they saw us as a subversive influence and we had to go. The problem was that we had nowhere to go and no money to go with. However, with no option but leaving we walked out carrying our bags and with our heads held high.

We had no idea where to go to and talked vaguely about finding the British Embassy. Phoning parents to ask for advice was ruled out because we feared it would cause untold anxiety and we wandered down the road towards the bar we had been visiting.

The bar proved to be our saviour, or rather the owner did. After we had drunk a glass or two of the Schlitz Draft Beer the barman sold, we unburdened ourselves to him. His response was far better than offering a free beer. He told us we could work for him and sleep in the bar until we got ourselves sorted. The only stipulation was that we did not tell anyone he was paying us and did not leave the bar after he locked it up at the end of the day's trading.

We served beer, washed dishes, delivered Pizzas and brushed the floor. Time flew by and we started to build up a reasonable amount of dollars in fact we almost had enough to get back to England. With hindsight we should have made our way home but if we had done so we would have missed a fantastic adventure, albeit one that could easily have put paid to a future Police career.

It was decided that we would go and have a look at Canada. I still do not know why we went North instead of South, perhaps it was as simple as the fact that the first Greyhound Bus to leave the New York terminal was going to Toronto. The scenery on the journey to Canada was spectacular and the journey passed smoothly.

Toronto in 1973 was a very clean city and a place that seemed to take itself very seriously. I lost count of the number of Canadians who told me that English people did not speak their own language properly. It was an offence to drink alcohol in public places and if you felt you had to do this then the only way to get away with it was to cover the can or bottle in a brown paper bag. There was absolutely no litter!

We stopped in a hostel in the central part of the city where we were advised to sleep with our wallets down our underpants and not leave anything movable lying around. We were woken after our first night by a bearded man asking if we wanted work and we explained our position as English visitors. This did not deter him and he explained that there were lots of blue-collar jobs that Canadians would not do. The answer was for us to make up a Canadian National Insurance Number and then leave before the number could be checked.

Our first day's work involved loading furniture from a warehouse into a fleet of vans. It was heavy work but well paid. After two or three days we decided to have a day off and do some sight-seeing. We found our way to the site of a recently held World Trade Show and then to Molson's' Brewery.

The Brewery trip was a great experience. Having seen the production line, visitors were allowed to sample the beers. There was a film show and small snacks to eat while sampling the brews. By ducking under a hatch, we managed to complete two tours and imbibe the full range of the company's products.

As we staggered back out into the daylight, I was aware that my legs were not totally under my control and I had an overwhelming urge to smile at everyone. As we crossed a wide roadway, I felt that paralysis had taken over. My left leg would not follow my right and I fell over. This would have been bad enough on a footpath but here vehicles were passing by in both directions and I was laying in the middle of the road. My companion came to my aid and helped me to my feet and it was only at that stage that I realized the stacked heel of my left shoe was stuck in a tram track. I tried to pull it out, oblivious to the approach of a tram on the same track. I got out of the way as the metal wheeled vehicle thundered past. As it moved away, I went to retrieve my shoe only to find that it was now almost two shoes. The trams wheel had sliced through the front of the shoe and only at the heel were the two halves connected.

Neither of us had a spare pair of footwear and I had to hobble back to the hostel that we were staying in. I tried to hold the shoe together with electricians insulating tape but it was a temporary job and eventually I had to spend a large chunk of my earnings on a new pair of shoes. It had been entirely my fault but somehow, I came to blame Toronto for the destruction of the shoe. It was time to move again and this time we knew where we were going. We were going to travel about a hundred miles from Toronto and get a job picking tobacco.

We had no real idea of how huge Canada is and when we arrived at a town in the tobacco growing area, we expected to be able to walk from farm to farm looking for work. The fact that some of the farms covered miles and miles of land had not occurred to us and we were extremely fortunate to meet a farmer in the first shop we visited. Mr Kormos not only had a farm but he was short of two workers for his four-man team. Accommodation and food would be provided in a bunk house and the pay was good with a bonus at the end of the season.

The scale of the country started to dawn on us as we were driven for over three hours along roads lined by identical farms and with not a hill in sight in any direction. On arrival we were introduced to the two workers who had already been recruited. These two were a little older than my companion and I. They were French Canadians from Montreal and at first, they seemed surly and unfriendly. As days merged one into another the icy relationship thawed and we became a real team.

Picking tobacco would rank as one of the worst jobs I have ever had. I have never had any urge to go and repeat the experience. The tobacco fields are huge and the plants are up to eight feet tall. Each picker sits on a metal seat similar to those found on old tractors. In front was metal container with three closed sides but open on that side facing the picker. There were four seats attached to the picking machine which consisted of a tractor like engine and four big wheels that ran between the rows of tobacco.

As the machine moved along the rows the picker plucked four or five leaves from the bottom of each plant and placed them in the container with the leaves pointed ends facing the direction of travel and the stalks facing the picker. It was extremely monotonous once you had mastered the speed which you had to pick at. The monotony was broken by the unpleasantness of the experience. In the morning there was often a chill in the air and a film of ice on some of the leaves. We wore as many clothes as possible under our waterproofs. By lunchtime it was so hot and steamy that you did not want to wear anything.

The mosquitoes arrived in swarms as soon as the air warmed. They were far bigger than the Mediterranean species and it actually hurt as they bit. Worst of all though was the nicotine. I had at this time no aversion to people who smoked and I quite liked to sniff pipe and cigar tobacco before they were lit. However, I soon found that the freshly picked leaves were very different from the dried and processed ones I had enjoyed. Every leaf and stem exuded large quantities of sap as they were parted from each other. Your fingers stuck together, the strands of your hair stuck together and even your eyelashes stuck together. This vile stuff turned black as the working day progressed and it was very difficult to remove, only soap impregnated with concrete as an abrasive seemed capable of getting it off. I regularly had to cut chunks of my hair off just so I could get a comb through what was left.

My time as a tobacco picker was also the first time, I was aware of blatant racism. My colleagues at the farm moved from incapable to barely competent in the time I was there, yet we were well treated, cleanly housed and very well fed. However, every morning, before we commenced picking, a team of Mississauga Indians were shipped in from a reservation to cut the suckers off the plants. They were paid a pittance, hardly spoken to and, it seemed, grudgingly given water. I am sure they would have been better pickers than I would ever have become but they were not allowed to. They were wonderful people; I lost my gold ring (made out of a sovereign left to me by my grandfather) while I was at the farm and they spent hours looking for it. I had never heard about Canadian Indians before my visit and I do not know if things have improved for them, I sincerely hope so. It was quite wrong that illegal workers were regarded as more employable than indigenous people.

It was the loss of the ring that persuaded me, yet again, that it was time to move on. My companion wanted to see out the season and secure the bonus but I had had enough of Canada. We had a day out to Niagara Falls to see if a break would make me feel differently. It did not. I thought Niagara was tacky, all Honeymoon Motels and trinket shops, plus the water had been turned off! After all this time I cannot remember quite what had happened but one side of the falls is used to generate electric and water is diverted. Whichever country did, whatever it had done, spoiled the experience. I wanted to go home.

The urge to go home may have been strong but an incident of naivety almost delayed that return. We made our apologies to Mr Kormos who justifiably felt we were letting him down mid-season and got a lift to the nearest town. There in a café we met four Americans who can only be described as hippies. They had long hair and two of them had large bushy moustaches. In discussion they said that they had been fruit picking and were now on their way back to the Florida Quays. They looked the sort of people who ride off into the sunset on Harley Davidson motor bikes but the reality was less exotic and they caught the same bus that we did.

My recollection of what happened next is a bit hazy but it went something like this. Our bus was due to cross the border between Canada and America at a place called Buffalo. Our new friends said that they were going to walk across the border to enjoy the view. They said that they would see us at the other side of the border where the bus stopped for an hour or so. Almost as an afterthought one of them asked if we would keep his bag with us so he did not have to walk with it. As they got off on the Canadian side of the border two uniformed Police Officers got on and started to check passports and belongings. I pulled the bag nearer us and saw that there was also a shoe box which I put on my knee. The officers, who may have been Immigration Officials and or Customs officers rather than police, arrived at our seats. When they found we were English they became quite chatty and extremely friendly. As they got off the bus, I placed the shoe box on an empty seat and as I did so the lid came off. It was absolutely full of herbal cannabis, dried leaves and seeds. I had just entered America with a drug cargo.!

There was no wonder our Florida bound friends were pleased to see us on the American side. I was in total shock, though the potential implications only dawned on me years later when I joined the Police and learned more about the penalties for doing what I had inadvertently done.

I was relieved to be going back to England, but even after the Canadian adventure we still did not have enough money to fly home. The solution again came to us in a bar. In America the medical system was essentially a private affair and clinics paid donors for giving blood. By giving a pint a day at different clinics and living frugally we could quickly amass enough to fly home. That is what we did though I would not recommend living on beer and boiled rice while giving blood as a means of funding the family holiday.

Having done so much in a relatively short period of time the return to England was something of an anti-climax. I still did not know what I wanted to do with my life. My mother felt I had come home with an American accent and, although no one else seemed to notice it, she was not happy. I certainly needed some cash and I applied for a job as a bus conductor to tide me over. I got the job but bowed to my father's assertion that "you're only as good as your last employment"; which was meant to tell me that I should be aiming at something better after having gained a Law Degree.

He may well have been right but the bus conducting could have given me some time to make a real decision about the future. Without the option of time, I started applying for positions as an Articled Clerk in Solicitor's Offices across the North of England. The quest resulted in my taking up a place with Messrs W. Formby and Son. Solicitors and Commissioners of Oaths.

As soon as I arrived at my new place of work, I wondered what I was there for. The premises were a throwback to Victorian times. Only two rooms in the whole building had shades on the lights, clerks sat on high stools behind raised desks and red ribboned files lay gathering dust on every surface. The senior partner was an eccentric figure who looked like he dressed from charity shops. He had long fingernails like talons, used snuff and smelled of urine. His office was heated by a coal fire which burned most of the day, though there was seldom more than a couple of pieces of fuel on it at any time.

The junior partner was small and slim with sunken cheeks and black oily hair that he brushed straight back from his forehead. He had a habit of wringing his hands as if in a state of perpetual despair. The office that he worked in was a cluttered mess of books and papers, one or two of which were more pornographic than legal.

My weekly pay was ten pounds and I found it impossible to make ends meet. I paid six pounds rent a week and lunch was seventy pence a day. It was not a matter of there being little slack left at the end of the week, rather a case of the last three days being completely devoid of funds. I started working behind the bar at the local rugby club and eventually at a small restaurant. However, if the pay was inadequate, it was, if I am wholly honest, probably more than I was worth.

The situation changed dramatically after about six months. A branch office was opened in a nearby market town and I was sent twice weekly to run this outpost of the Formby empire. This would not be allowed nowadays as a fully qualified solicitor would have to be present and I was certainly not that. The work was more interesting and I did not tell people that I was not yet what they thought I was.

On one occasion I was visited by a lady who had had to close her green grocery business. The front entrance to her shop opened onto a busy street and the rear door led to an enclosed yard. The local council required her to be able to dispose of refuse without bringing it through the shop. She was heartbroken and wanted to know what could be done. In talking she told me that there had been a greengrocer's shop in those premises for many years before she took over the business. This piece of information started the cogs moving in my brain and I spent time in the council offices and the town library. There had indeed been a shop there for at least fifty years but more importantly the bye law regarding refuse was at least that old, there must once have been a way out through the rear yard.

On one side the yard boundary was a house wall, on the other was a Public House trading under the name of the Crown. The Crown had belonged to Rose's Brewery but had been taken over by a large modern company in fairly recent years. It transpired that the new company had closed a gap in the wall from the greengrocer's yard which had allowed access to the car park at the back of the pub. They had then built a bottle store where an access used to be. After lots of research I found two old dustbin men who remembered collected the green grocer's vegetable waste from bins on the pub car park. It proved possible to establish a right of way and reluctantly the brewery allowed the greengrocer to reopen the gap in her wall. Her business was allowed to re-open and she was delighted.

Formby's managed to bill the shop keeper for the princely sum of sixteen hundred pounds. This seemed like a good time to ask for a pay rise, so I did. The result was that the junior partner gave me a free fifty pence ticket to the jazz club that he helped run. Something had to give and in a moment of impulse I walked out never to return.

In later years as I came to understand more about the world and the relevance of civil law, I think I might have made a fairly useful solicitor, at the time a parting of the ways was probably the right course for both sides. It left me out of work and even worse off financially than before. I continued with the bar work and also got a job working in a fish and chip shop.

One strange event that took place at this time is worth recounting because it links to the future and my time in the Police. The rugby club I worked at and played for was a very social entity and attracted lots of heavy drinkers from the neighbourhood. There was also a card playing and gambling school which met in a windowless committee room. When the bar closed at the end of a nights trading the real players got started. They tipped me to keep serving booze as they gambled the night and the early hours of the next day away. It often went on until two and three o' clock in the morning and sometimes there would be scuffles and accusations of cheating.

One night after everyone had left and I had locked the club and set the alarm I noticed something in the hedge at the side of the carpark. It turned out to be one of the men who had been playing cards earlier. I had not seen him leave and here he was lying half in and half out of a privet hedge. He was comatose and very cold but snoring gently in his stupor. I could have left him there but I tried to wake him without success. This was before the time of mobile phones so ringing the police was not an option. I checked his pockets in the hope of finding an address. His driving licence was in his wallet and his house was only some quarter of a mile away. I put him over my shoulder and set off. It was heavy work but not too bad after months of rugby training.

The house was in darkness, nobody answered the bell or my knocking but the door was open so I took him in, laid him on the sofa in his living room and left a note saying what I had done. I felt like a good Samaritan as I walked back to my flat and expected at least a complimentary pint the next time the man came to the club. Imagine my surprise when I opened the door the following morning to find two police officers standing there.

In a nutshell I was accused of taking money from the man's wallet. My flat was searched even though I told them there was little chance of finding money anywhere near me. They took me to the police station and started to tell me I would be charged with theft and that the onus would be on me to prove I had not taken the money. At last, the legal training kicked in and I pointed out that in reality they would have to prove beyond reasonable doubt that I had taken the money. This did not go down well, they clearly did not like being corrected and they tried another tack. The man I had found was an off-duty police detective and the court would obviously believe him before me. I was really worried; my father was a serving police officer in another Force and I already felt I had let him down by walking out of the solicitors. Just being accused of being a thief felt like an unjust slur. I was bailed and allowed to go back to my flat. As I made my way home, I felt that everyone was looking at me. When I got inside the flat, I did not feel like going out again.

Fortunately, however, I broke the spell of inaction and made my way back to the club for another night's work. It was quiet and I helped the Steward clean the shelves and polish the glasses while we waited for customers. He must have realized something was wrong and in response to his asking why I was so quiet I blurted out all that had happened. As soon as he heard what I had to say he was able to offer me some light at the end of the tunnel.

"You can't have taken his money, cos he didn't have any left. He was well pissed and losing every hand. He wanted to bet his watch but no one would take it and he staggered off broke, long before the rest of us left."

The tension seemed to drain away and I wanted to ring the police straight away. I didn't do that though and was a bit surprised when the officers I had seen earlier walked into the club. By closing time, they had spoken to a number of people who were able to confirm what the Steward had said and while the officers mumbled about illegal gambling, they said I would be released from my bail.

I did see the man again but not at the rugby club. When I saw him again, he was a detective inspector in the Police Force I went on to join. We had a further run in and that is why I have spent time outlining this incident here. In my opinion he was a music hall type villain but you can make your own mind up later.

Certainly, my brush with the powers of law and order did not send me the message that I must rush off and join the nearest constabulary. I never really considered joining at that time even though my degree did seem wasted on bar work. Instead, I joined FW Woolworth as a trainee manager and I enjoyed almost every minute of it.

Nowadays, Woolworth's stores have disappeared from the UK high street but for most of the twentieth century you could find them everywhere. They owned most of the sites that their stores stood on and as these were prime positions in busy towns and cities they were worth a fortune. The top managers were very well paid and the salaries were not a secret.

I started work in a fairly large store with about sixty staff and its own canteen and large warehouse. The job was diverse, ranging from ordering correct stock levels, ensuring the goods were attractively displayed and bannered and ensuring that cleaners and delivery men did what they were supposed to. It also involved tasks that were not included in the job description, like displaying fruit and vegetables, boning sides of bacon, operating the cooked meat slicer and filling in for anyone who did not turn up. I was often the best dressed toilet cleaner in the area.

I must admit that I enjoyed catching shop lifters. Woolworth's regarded the loss of goods through theft, breakages and deterioration as 'shrinkage'. That is, profits shrunk from expected levels because goods were not sold. Catching thieves was good fun and a break from the mundane but it got me into trouble every now and then.

On one occasion I was chatting with a member of staff who was working on the sweet counter. As we talked, I saw a tall, scruffy man lingering by the frozen food fridge. As I watched he selected a frozen chicken and examined it from every possible angle. He then pushed it up the tatty purple jumper that he was wearing. It was so blatant that I was momentarily transfixed by his audacity. The man walked past me and towards the front door of the shop. I set off in pursuit and he must have realized that he had been seen because he set off running down the busy street outside the shop.

Now I like to think that in my early twenties I was quite fleet of foot but the man with the chicken up his jumper was faster. This could turn out to be embarrassing, several staff members had seen me run out of the store and I could not go back without the thief. I chased him up alleyways and down streets until at last he started to slow and then, nearing exhaustion, I rugby tackled him as he crossed a busy dual carriageway. There was a crunch and a crack which I assumed to be the frozen chicken hitting the road. However, as I dragged the man to his feet it was obvious that he was not well. I almost carried him back to the store which was not pleasant as he stunk of stale alcohol and B.O. Fortunately, he was too shattered to try and escape as I was carrying the battered chicken as well as him.

Back in the store I waited for the Police to arrive and during this time I realized that I had torn my suit trousers and grazed the knuckles of my right hand. The man did not seem any better, he sat huddled up staring at the floor and moaning every time he breathed. After I had been to the Police Station the man was taken to the hospital where he was found to have two broken ribs and a chipped elbow. There was some discussion about whether or not I had exercised only reasonable force in detaining him. It was certainly clear that the police officers were not pleased at having to do full interviews for the theft of a chicken and they kept me sweating for days before telling me I would not be prosecuted for assault.

The store manager reluctantly agreed to have my trousers 'invisibly' mended but there was no reward and not even a mention in the staff weekly newsletter. However, I was to be no more impressed by the management at Marks and Spencer's when I tried to help them.

One evening as I waited for the bus that would convey me back to my lodgings, I decided to buy a bar of chocolate. I often went into Marks' shop to check if they were selling things more cheaply than we were and I was known to some of their management. As I looked at the different chocolate bars available, I saw a man with a cello case stood nearby. He was bearded, had long hair and wore a black hat. As I watched him, he picked up a handful of sweet packets and paced them on his cello case, when I looked back the sweets were gone. This was like magic and the trick was repeated with several blocks of cheese at the dairy counter. There was obviously a hole in the case and he was pushing things through it.

I looked for someone from the store's management team without success and as the man left the shop, I grabbed him and his case. The cello case did indeed have a hole in the side, a very professional job with a flap on a hinge. Inside the case was an Aladin's' cave of stolen goods. I thought I had hit the jackpot; this was professional theft and I had saved Marks' a good amount of money and there were goods from other stores. But if I expected a pat on the back, it was not forthcoming.

Mark's let the man go and allowed him to take his cello case with him. The police were not called and when I went to work the following day I was summoned before my manager. The reason for my presence in Marks and Spencer's had been questioned and basically the message was don't interfere where you are not wanted. I never bought chocolate from them again though I remained partial to their sandwiches......principles only go so far!

I worked in three other Woolworth's stores ending up as temporary manager at Seacroft on the outskirts of Leeds. Then I applied for a post as assistant Personnel Manager at the company's headquarters in Dudley. I was not successful, ostensibly because I could not drive at the time. However, the interviewer must have been taken with me because he rang a few days later to offer me my own store. It was in Birmingham and I went to look. Now I am hopeful that someone from Birmingham may one day read what I am writing and I do not want to upset them but I could not wait to get out of the place. The question was how did I turn down the very thing I was supposed to have been working for.?

The answer was surprisingly easy. I left the company and joined the Police.

CHAPTER 4

UPWARDS AND ONWARDS

Joining the Police was not as easy as I expected. No sooner had I submitted the application form than a Police Sergeant arrived on my doorstep. There was no warning that I would be receiving a visit and I was completely unprepared. I suppose that was the whole point of it. I later saw reports that "home visit" interviewers submitted and they contained comments like, "respectable but working-class dwelling, clean and properly maintained" or "untidy, one bedroomed flat, clearly not house proud". The questions that I was asked would no longer be considered politically correct either. My visitor openly asked if I was a homosexual, why I did not live with my parents, whether I had any friends with criminal records, it went on and on. All I could think was that I wished I had had the chance to tidy up and put some clean socks on.

The initial process was unpleasant but it must have gone reasonably well as I soon received a letter inviting me to a formal selection interview at Police Headquarters. For that I was able to make sure I had had a wash and put my suit on. The questions were easier and I got the impression that the Police wanted me. The interviewing officers seemed very impressed that I had a Law Degree and came from a police background. They were quite honest about the fact that the Force was considerably understrength and they were recruiting heavily. It did not seem to be a case of them selecting me but rather sending me a "Please Join" message.

At the time of my applying to join the entire Police Service was struggling to attract and hold on to new recruits. Pay and conditions had fallen behind those of other jobs. An enquiry had been commissioned by the Government to look into what was needed. The resulting report became known as the 'Edmund Davies Report', its official title is probably long forgotten. However, when I was interviewed the report was only recently submitted and definitely not accepted. I was joining another job where the pay was going to be low, albeit I hoped it would be liveable.

My official acceptance came through within a very short period of time and Christmas 1977 was to be my last as a civilian for over thirty years.

The Police Headquarters that I reported to was a 1960's glass and concrete construction. It was shaped like a shoe box with no adorning towers or gables, just a tall radio aerial projecting from the roof. At the rear there was a narrow parking area, petrol pumps and a garage workshop. The whole police building was overlooked from the rear by a large council owned multi storey car park. The front of the building looked out onto gardens and then the local Town Hall.

I had been in police buildings before when visiting with my father, however, for most of the new recruits that I joined with the whole first day seemed to be a magical mystery tour. The only mystery to me was the presence of an individual I had nicknamed 'Wolf' when I met him at the pre selection medical. This individual was a smaller version of the actor Brian Blessed, he had a thick beard and crinkly, black wavy hair. Portly in build his thick forearms suggested great strength. In spite of his build Wolf had failed the eyesight test, one part of which required a candidate to pick out numbers coloured a certain shade from a background of different shades of the same colour. Wolf was colour blind, the task was impossible for him and as my group of selection candidates dressed and left the Doctor's surgery Wolf was still there in his underpants.

"How did you make it?" I asked genuinely perplexed.

"Well officially I passed at the second attempt." He replied and then continued, "In reality the Doc took me out into the gardens and pointed at the grass then asked me what colour it was. I got that right and also the colour of the top light on a set of traffic lights".

Any illusion that I had joined a finely honed band of crime fighters started to fade from this point and only the free canteen food prevented the day sinking into anti-climax.

The whole point of us being at Headquarters was to familiarize us with our own Force; to issue us with uniforms and to swear us in as constables before we were sent away to Police Regional Training School for thirteen weeks of drill, theory and 'practical's'. The issue of uniform was a farce as our motley crew tried to fit into the proffered clothing. My trousers fit, provided I tightened a piece of string underneath my belt which was too big and my helmet resembled a bucket with a large chrome nipple on the top.

We were allowed a whole morning to learn the oath that we had to swear to the Queen in front of a local magistrate. Police Officers are Crown Servants and we had to swear to serve the Queen. We were then taken to an impressive wood panelled courtroom and one by one we had to stand in the witness box and with one hand on the Bible recite the Oath. Some of my group needed several attempts which again diluted the solemnity of the occasion but eventually we were released for a final weekend before commencing the training course.

I had got to know one or two of the others quite well during our induction at Police Headquarters. One of them, Steve, was an ex-soldier and he had agreed to give me a lift to the Training School which was miles from anywhere. Steve arrived on Sunday night with military precision and he helped me carry my suitcase and bag to his car. The only problem was that there were two other people already in the vehicle which was an old Mini. Altogether there were four of us and four suitcases together with miscellaneous bags and carriers.

To this day I do not know how we made it. The car smelled of exhaust fumes and the engine screamed and stuttered on every incline. I am sure we never went faster than thirty miles an hour but eventually we rolled to a halt on the car park at the school. It was based in a partially closed RAF Station. After leaving our belongings in a designated dormitory we were told to report to the Dining Room.

There were about eighty student constables from a number of northern Police Forces. The atmosphere was one of apprehension but there was also a buzz of forced jollity and general chit chat. I noticed four uniformed sergeants enter; they were wearing caps with the peaks slashed so that they came down over the foreheads of the wearers in a very militaristic way. Each of them carried a military 'swagger stick'. They quietly positioned themselves in the corners of the dining room. No one else seemed to have noticed them or maybe everyone just expected to see police sergeants at a police training school. Very few of us could have expected the shouting and abuse that suddenly erupted from the four corners of the room.

"Stand up," shouted one sergeant. "Sit down," shouted another.

"They don't know what sitting means do they?" Asked one.

"They do not." Replied another.

"They are horrible are they not?"

All four then agreed that the assembled recruits were indeed horrible.

This bombardment went on for about ten minutes. A girl standing near me was crying and holding her handkerchief to her face.

"There's one who won't make it Sergeant Davies." Shouted a small rotund sergeant.

"Indeed, she will not Sergeant Jones." Came a reply from the other corner of the room.

The sobbing girl did not make it. She left the same night and two more left the following morning. It seemed a pointless exercise and I can only assume that those who departed were deemed to be lacking in moral fibre. I had done my fair share of walking out of jobs but the shouting had little impact. It seemed in some ways that I was watching a film that I was appearing in and the Sergeants were the villains. They never made me feel I had to leave, though the freezing cold, both in and outside, made continued survival questionable!

I found the marching and drilling hard work, my coordination did not seem to fit, but I was nowhere near as bad as some individuals who walked like robots and kept going when the command to halt was given. Cross country running across frozen fields was quite enjoyable, certainly more so than the cold showers which we had to take on completion of the runs. It was also a requirement that we could swim well enough to pass lifesaving examinations, this was going to be a problem as I could not swim at all!

As a child I had eczema quite badly. When I went to primary school my mother used to bandage my knees so that the open and weeping eczema sores did not get infected. Life can be cruel and the first time the bandages came loose I was followed by groups of children calling me "Leper" and other equally unpleasant names. The result was that I never enjoyed going to swimming pools and taking my clothes off. By the time I reached Grammar School the eczema was just about gone and I remember being involved in fund raising to help the school build its own pool. I had, however, never learned to swim.

The Police Training School did not have its own pool, we had to travel and the adventure started as soon as soon as we got up. Swimming might have been regarded as important to the trainers, but it was not important enough to be programmed into the normal working day. We had to get up at five in the morning so that we could have a cup of sweet tea before setting off for the pool at six o' clock. We were loaded onto bus which if it had been based in Malta would have been an antique tourist attraction. There was no discernible heating, the seating area filled with exhaust fumes almost immediately we set off and on occasion the whole back window fell out. I am sure the bus did have the relevant documents and met required safety standards but it would not have taken much evidence to persuade me otherwise.

Half gassed and so cold that it was difficult to get your clothes off we arrived at the ancient pool. The water was not particularly warm either but it was just about bearable; less tolerable were the massive drips of icy condensation which fell from the glass panels in the ceiling of the pool building. They would splatter on you when you least expected it often taking your breath away. As the weeks went by the trips became more tolerable and the antics that recruits got up to showed we were becoming hardened to the conditions.

If you climbed on to the shower room wall adjacent to the Gents Changing Room you could see into the Female Changing Room. This was considered great fun and people used to queue for their turn. One of the girls became something of a legend, apparently her pubic hair grew down the inside of her legs towards her knees. She also had large breasts and I am sure many fantasies were launched in the crumbling pool house. Sadly, the same girl became pregnant during the course; this was not necessarily a scandal even in the cloistered world of the training school. However, the fact that the father to be was one of the Training Sergeants who had welcomed us on our first night caused some amusement. I am sure he struggled to explain his return home to his wife.!

I never became a great swimmer but I managed to pass the exams and fortunately I never had to rescue anyone from water in my entire career.

There were few adventures that I can remember from my time at training school. It snowed heavily during January and we were cut off from the rest of the world, literally and psychologically. The events of the real World seemed to belong to another time and dimension. For us the big issues were making sure our shoes were shiny, trousers pressed and knowledge of the criminal law up to scratch. While we sat in classrooms learning definitions off by heart RAF training was also going on, planes landed and immediately took off again. It was, I believe, called 'Circuits and Bumps' and for us it could be strangely hypnotic. The days passed as if in a trance for most and yet our numbers were dwindling. One of the officers from my Force never came back from a weekend at home having been caught shoplifting, others just left because they could not stand any more of it.

The most exciting thing from my point of view was being called to see the Commandant of the Training School. I had no idea why he wanted to see me. He was someone you only saw at parades or if you were in serious trouble. I could not understand why I was in serious trouble and worried that something might have happened to my parents. The mystery was not completely resolved when I left the Commandants Office, he informed me that my Chief Constable wanted to see me. I was given a time and date when I had to report to my Force Headquarters but then, to my amazement, I was asked what it was all about!

I am not certain that anyone believed I had no idea why I had been called to Headquarters. Some assumed that it must be a disciplinary issue that I would not talk about. Some thought I was being sent on an undercover operation. All I knew was that I had to catch a train, change twice and be at Headquarters in full uniform. The Commandant arranged for a car to take me to the local railway station and the rest was up to me. As I got out of the warm car it was snowing big fluffy flakes and the platform was deserted. A train did arrive and I made my destination on time.

I entered Headquarters through the front door, forgetting I had been issued with a 'Box Key' that opened all doors into the building. The Chief Constables' suite of offices was on the first floor and I made my way there up the stairs. As I approached the swing doors that led to the seat of power, I heard someone calling. A small man in a checked brown suite was making his way towards me and almost jogging as he sought to close the distance between us.

"You are PC Marchbank, aren't you?" He asked and seemed relieved when I said I was.

"Thank goodness I've caught you. You must be wondering why you're here I bet?"

I told him that I had no idea why I had been called and he asked me to accompany him to an office nearby. There, as I watched the clock on his wall tick towards my appointment time, he told me why I was there. It was both strange and mundane, exciting yet anti-climactic in the same instance. The man was a senior civilian working in the Force's Personnel Branch. He had been asked to identify anyone in the Force who may be eligible for the Accelerated Promotion Scheme that the Home Office ran. He had struggled to find many candidates and noticed that I had a degree and had only just joined. He had, therefore, put my name forward and when I was accepted as meeting the initial criteria, he had also completed the application form on my behalf. I was present at Headquarters for the first interview to see if I was suitable for the scheme. So much for preparation time!

I have never been quite certain if this small man, who I came to know quite well, had done me a favour or a disservice. I had joined the Police to be a police officer, I had not joined because I felt I had a Chief Constable's Baton in my back pocket. I had needed a job but I was, as I have explained, deeply suspicious of the Police hierarchy and the way they operated. From this point on, if I was successful, I would be marked as someone different and one message I had learned at training school was that it is best not to stand out. It was better to be third or fourth than first or last. The extremes got picked out for bullying by the Drill Sergeants or performing the practical exercises in front of visiting Chief Officers.

Anyway, there will be more about the Accelerated Promotion Scheme later, for now suffice it to say that the Chief Constable put me forward for the next round of selection and I was packed off back to training school. There, the warm food continued to be supplied in large amounts, the bar continued to open on an evening and the parading served to burn the calories off.

As the snow thawed our sporting ventures become more adventurous. The rugby team from my own Force visited and I played against them. It was a hard game and was very definitely in the coarse rugby category of game. The beer afterwards was more fun than acquiring the scratches and bruises that the game brought. I was greeted like a long lost relative by the opposition, once they found out I was joining them. I was given phone numbers, all sorts of information and an invitation to go on the Force rugby tour which was set to take place two weeks after I had returned from training.

I enjoyed the evening so much that I paid a deposit for the tour before my new colleagues set off back. Only later did I wonder if I should have settled into policing before I took off to play rugby in Wales. Beer does have a tendency to dull the intellect as well as aid relaxation and temporarily remove worries!

I will finish this rugby interlude here because it will soon be time for real Police things and I do not want to be distracted. We set off on tour with two Chief Inspectors along to make sure we behaved. There was a crate of beer at the back of the bus and that lasted for the first twenty or thirty miles of the journey. From that stage it is a moot point as to whether we stopped most frequently to buy more beer or to get rid of that which we had drunk. We arrived in Blaenavon late and spent the evening playing bar games in the local rugby club. One of these games involved kneeling with a bottle in each hand and then seeing how far you could stretch forward, deposit one bottle and get back to your starting point using the other one. This simple pursuit cost us a valuable player when the neck of a bottle broke and the resultant injury required several stitches at the local hospital.

After an extremely vicious game of rugby, we went to Cardiff for an evening out. Now, I have visited Cardiff several times in recent years and really like the place, but my memories of the visit in 1978 are very different. I remember Brains' Beer with big white lumps at the bottom of the glass, surly people in dingy pubs and miles of grim, dirty houses. It was as we wandered along one stretch of road lined by semi derelict buildings that I felt a crunching blow to the back of my head. I cannot then remember anything for a little while until I became aware that I was sitting on the footpath with my back against a car. Blood was trickling down my neck and the collar of my shirt was quite wet with it.

It transpired that I had been shot in the head. Fortunately, this was not a gangland hit on a feared crime fighter, rather it was a teenager with an air rifle who had managed to hit the thickest part of my anatomy….my skull. When I touched the growing lump on the back of my head, I could feel the metal pellet sticking out of my scalp. Two of my colleagues had run off to try and find the rifleman while others were looking for a police officer. As I stood up, with my head thumping, a police car pulled up and the driver got out. My account of what he said is a best attempt bearing in mind his accent, my wound and several pints of beer, but it was something like,

"What are you doing hanging round these cars?"

We explained we were a rugby team on a 'pub crawl' and that I had just been shot. He replied,

"Well, it's your own fault coming down here, you don't belong, see?"

We asked what we should do and what he was going to do and he said,

"You should Fuck Off out of here and that's what I will be doing"

Then he got in his car and, good as his word, he drove off into the night. So, I never figured in Cardiff's' Crime Statistics, nor did I avail myself of the local branch of the NHS. A rugby player called Geoff removed the pellet with a pocket knife and someone else put some whisky on the wound. As we made our way back to the centre of Cardiff someone pointed out helpfully,

"You've still got a head. What more do you want!"

Anyway, I still had all that to look forward to as we came towards the close of our course. I did not win the award for the best marcher; I did not win the Commandants Award for the Best Academic Student and I was not Sports person of the Course. I was, however, the only student to dare to ask the female inspector in charge of training for a dance and somehow this seemed to attract great praise. As we drove away from the training school it began to dawn that we were leaving a safe environment and about to become real police officers!

CHAPTER FIVE

THE REAL WORLD

I was due to start my first tour of duty as a police officer at 23.00 hours (11 pm) and I had been told that I should be in the station and ready for briefing at least quarter of an hour before that time. So, I entered through the northernmost door of the building using my box key. Letting myself into the station gave me quite a buzz but that only lasted until I entered the Parade Room.

A parade room was a place where officers coming on duty gathered to be told what areas (beats) they would be working, what activities they should look out for on the areas, together with a list of stolen vehicles and 'wanted' people who may be found there. Those officers who were going off duty would also arrive in the Parade Room to hand over the keys for their cars or to pass on any information that had come to light during the previous shift.

In later years I attended parades in other Police Forces and found them to be very different from what I experienced on my first night and subsequently. In West Yorkshire, for example, officers had to stand to attention when the inspector entered the room and they were then inspected. Their boots had to be clean, their accoutrements (equipment) were checked and notebooks had to be produced to prove that they were up to date.

As I walked into the parade room on my first night, I was surprised how laid back everyone was. Very few of those present were wearing full uniform with tunic jackets fastened. Some were leaning back in their chairs with their feet on the central table. The room was very warm and even after the sergeant had finished his briefing there seemed to be little rush to get out onto the streets, in fact cups of tea started to appear as if by magic; there was a background of chit chat and a radio playing quietly.

Nowadays officers often put themselves on duty at remote locations and on occasion they might not see another colleague during an entire shift. The public often ask at meetings and in letters to newspapers where all the police officers have gone. I will comment on their disappearance later in these pages but for now I can report that on my first night there were seven car beats with each car 'manned' by at least one officer and there were also ten officers to cover each of the foot beats that comprised the sub division to which I was attached. These numbers were not regularly achieved due to shortfalls in recruitment, sickness and abstractions to other duties such as court appearances.

The officers mentioned above represented the operational strength of our 'relief'. There were four reliefs at the sub division and at any time one would be working early turn(mornings), the second would be on 'Lates'(evenings) and the third would cover nights while the fourth would be taking their days off. Each relief also had at least two operational sergeants and an inspector; then there would be a sergeant and three constables in the control room and a sergeant and a constable in the custody office (where prisoners were received and kept in custody). There was also a smattering of civilian staff who helped perform many of the inside 'station duties'.

For now, I think that is enough technical information. Peter James the crime fiction writer says that police officers often fall back on "Plod Speak" when they start reminiscing. I will do my best not to, but for me a little of it should add atmosphere and background knowledge.

When people started to wander out of the parade room, I began to realize that I had not been given anything to do and it was becoming clear that no one was going to come to my rescue. I went to find the sergeant who clearly did not know I was coming and had not noticed me amongst the others. This was a low-key start if ever there was one. I had achieved total anonymity and could have gone home without anyone being much the wiser. As he realized he had overlooked me the sergeant recovered his equilibrium, the omission was clearly my fault. I should, he said, have spoken up and asked for a job, now it was difficult because everyone was deployed. He told me there was no one still on the station who could take me out on duty with them, though I knew the parade room was still half full. As a favour he told me that he would call a Traffic Officer and ask him to show me round the Force area.

Within minutes blue lights were flashing outside the window of the sergeant's office and a short time later a sandy haired, fairly rotund and red-faced police officer presented himself to us. This officer had a white cover on the top of his cap and this identified him as a member of the Traffic Division. After a brief chat between the new arrival and the sergeant I found myself escorted to a Ford Granada Police Traffic Car, the blue lights of which were still flashing.

"We'll have to get a move on." My new friend stated. "I didn't know you were coming. What's your night vision like?"

I told him I could see quite well in the dark and we roared off into the night with horns blaring and lights flashing. As we left the urban sprawl of the city, the lights and two tones were switched off but the speed, if anything, increased. The traffic driver seemed lost in concentration and I did not interrupt him, trees flashed by regularly in the beams of the car's lights along with the occasional farm house.

After about twenty minutes we entered a village and our speed slowed. The driver then switched of the engine and the lights of our car and we freewheeled down a hill before coming to a halt behind a police dog handlers van and the local beat officers Ford Escort. We left the car and walked towards an open garage that faced directly onto the road, then we clambered up a grassy bank at the side of the garage onto a ridge that overlooked a large ornate garden. Standing in the shadows of a clump of rhododendron bushes we came across the officers from the other vehicles.

I was beginning to get quite excited by now. It seemed that I was to be involved in a memorable operation on my first night and this feeling was reinforced when a fourth vehicle pulled up on the road behind us. In the gloom I could see the shape of a large house set back in the gardens. As I allowed my eyesight to adjust a light came on in the upper part of the house. I could quite clearly see a woman enter the room and stand near the window, she then began to undress and the dog handler retrieved a small pair of binoculars from his coat pocket. The woman continued to undress until it was obvious, she was completely naked. There was a general grabbing for the binoculars and as this progressed the dog handler slipped on the wet earth where we were standing and fell backwards onto the roof of the garage. There was a loud crash and then a horrendous shriek as the asbestos roof split and the falling officer disappeared into the bowels of the garage. I looked towards the house and it was obvious that the lady had heard the commotion she was standing, still naked, peering out into the darkness.

The beat officer was the first to react. Having regained his car, he accelerated off into the night with his blue light flashing. The rest of us were not far behind him as we all sought to put distance between us and the house. We could, as my driver pointed out, only hope that the lady had not been able to see anything in the darkness. Moments later we received a call on the radio asking us to attend the very house we had just fled from.

Sheepishly we knocked on the large blue door of the dark house. The lady who I had seen earlier without clothes now opened the door wearing a thick dressing gown, she invited us in. Several minutes later, drinking a cup of tea in China cups she recounted the strange events from her point of view. She suggested someone had tried to break into the garage but thought that the would-be thieves must have been drunk as the garage was open and obviously empty. My colleague who was now standing warming the backs of his legs in the heat from an open log fire assured the lady she was probably correct and very perceptive. I was amazed by how casual he was and ultimately staggered when I realized that he kept adjusting his position to get a better view of the lady's cleavage, which had been revealed by her dressing gown slipping open.

We informed the lady that we would keep a look out in the area and submit the appropriate paperwork regarding the damage to the garage roof. Only then did she drop the bombshell on us, "I am sure they'll be caught. I saw a blue light flashing immediately after the crash. Perhaps you've got them already"

"I am sure they'll be apprehended." Ventured the traffic officer and we scurried down the drive back to our car. Nothing ever came of the incident, we got away with it but I have often wondered on how many nights impromptu strips had been witnessed from the grassy mound. Did the lady know all along that she had been watched? I never went back to find out. I was relieved to have escaped any disciplinary repercussions and that was all that I can remember happening on my first night.

When I joined my chosen Police Force, they required unmarried new recruits to live in lodgings or 'digs' as they were most commonly known. My digs were in a rough part of the city, there was a bail hostel around the corner and most houses were occupied by students. However, if the house was in a poor location, Mrs. Jennings kept the inside of the dwelling in immaculate condition. She was of Polish origin and Mr Jennings was an ice cream man whose van was the newest and cleanest vehicle on the street.

It took me nearly half an hour to walk from the police station to my lodgings and I was almost dreaming of bed. I let myself in with the key that had been given me when I had called earlier. The house was quiet and I climbed the stairs to my bedroom where I eagerly clambered into the bed. I must have drifted off to sleep because the noise of banging on the bedroom door gave me a start like an electric shock. As I came round the door opened and Mrs. Jennings walked in.

"Ah! Ben James you are here." She announced.

I never found out what 'ben' meant but she used it before anyone's name.

"Your breakfast is waiting!"

I did not want breakfast; I had been in bed nearly an hour and the thought of getting up was not a pleasant one. Nevertheless, I followed her down to the kitchen area where a full, fried English breakfast was waiting for me. I felt a bit nauseous at the thought of eating but at the same time I did not want to get off on a bad footing with my landlady. The breakfast did look quite good and Mrs Jennings wandered off to clean and prepare her husbands' ice cream van. Appearances were, however, deceptive. The top side of every item on my plate was barely cooked, the bottoms of the same items were burned. I found out later that the cooking technique involved putting everything in a pan, lighting the gas and then going to do another job somewhere else. On this occasion I managed to put most of the uncooked, burned offerings in the bin. I was not always so lucky.

The morning adventure was not yet over. I now felt wide awake even though I had had less than an hour's sleep. I decided to unpack my bag which was exactly where I had placed it on arrival. I put socks and underpants in a chest of drawers and my jumpers and jackets in the wardrobe. Above the last piece of furniture was a cupboard high in the wall. I stretched up to open the doors and as I did so a pair of black boots fell out of the cupboard and struck me a glancing blow on the side of my head.

On examination I found the boots to be Doc Martins, size eleven and highly polished. As I looked at them a drop of blood fell from my head onto the shiny leather. I was bleeding quite a lot and holding a handkerchief on the wound did not seem to do much good. Mr Jennings took me to the Hospital in his ice cream van and when, after being stitched up, I returned to his parking place he was busy selling ice cream to patients.

Back at the lodgings Mrs. Jennings spent nearly an hour telling me that the boots belonged to "Ben Paul" who had occupied the room before me. Paul Smith was to figure regularly during my career, he was the officer who frightened me on the way to the firearms incident in Chapter One. It would be easy to digress and tell a few tales about Smithy who was something of a legend even then but I will put that off for now. At the time I just wanted to go back to bed and I did, at least until teatime when I was woken up again.

The second night at work was initially a little more organized. I was paired up with another officer on a foot beat near to the station. We wandered up and down a number of streets, looked in the darkened windows of a few pubs and chatted generally about football and rugby. The radio was quiet and the only thing that happened in the first three hours was that a sergeant came to visit us and checked that our notebooks were up to date. I reckoned keeping the notebooks up to date should be would be easy if every night was as quiet as this.

Then, as I was mentally dozing off, things started to happen. We were sent to the location of an assault. To get there involved a fairly long walk but no one gave us any indication that the situation was urgent. When we arrived in the general area that the assault was supposed to have taken place, we could find no sign of anyone. We spread our search out and eventually, under a large concrete flyover, we found the body of a middle-aged man. He was lying in a large pool of blood; his skin was cold and I feared that he was dead. No one had called an ambulance and we rectified that.

The man had no means of identification in any of his pockets. As we looked round the area, we found a wallet but it was completely empty. We also noticed that on a support of the flyover, close to the prostrate man, was a red smudge and a piece of something of indeterminate origin. I told my colleague that I believed the object was part of the victim's scalp.

Within a few minutes the ambulance arrived and took the injured man to hospital. The scenes of crime officers came and did an initial investigation in the dark. The wallet went into a brown paper evidence envelope. A detective constable came next, he smelled of stale beer and smoke but he arranged for the area to be cordoned off and told me he thought I was right about the scalp. The warm glow of being pronounced to be a "thinker" did not last long. I was to remain at the scene by myself and make sure no one interfered with anything.

Only now did I start to realize how cold it was and how quiet this area was. My fingers soon went numb and I became bored with walking round and round in circles. As the night progressed it seemed to get colder and on this and later occasions, I formed the opinion that the coldest time was just before dawn. Nobody contacted me to see if I was alright, no other human being ventured anywhere nearby and I couldn't even hear any vehicles on the flyover.

When my relief came, they found me stood against a support of the flyover apparently fast asleep. I certainly felt dazed and not a hundred percent certain where I was. Fortunately, the piece of scalp was still attached to the concrete, everything was as it had been when we found it. By the time I next came on duty the culprits had been arrested and charged. The man had gone to a nightclub and taken up with a woman who agreed to have sex with him under the flyover. As they prepared for the moment of pleasure the womans boyfriend came up from behind and smashed the man' head against the concrete. The culprits then emptied the man's wallet and made off. The boyfriend was known to the police and identified by his fingerprints on the wallet. The victim recovered.

I survived a second breakfast at the Jennings' and actually slept for five hours or so. When I woke up, I did not feel too good, I had headache, indeed everything seemed to ache and I still felt cold. Nevertheless, by work time I put my uniform on and set off to the station. The night was quiet again with little radio traffic and few people on the streets but that was to change dramatically. I started to pick up messages about a rape that had taken place in a nearby park. I started to make my way there even though strictly speaking it was off the beat I had been allocated.

On my arrival at the scene of the rape there were police officers everywhere, detectives were visiting houses in the vicinity in the hope that someone had heard or seen something. The actual location of the alleged offence was a flower bed behind some public toilets. There was no lighting in the vicinity and everyone was waiting for a search light. The victim was at the hospital where she was, according to a fellow constable, refusing to submit herself to an examination. No one seemed to have anything for me to do and, indeed, I seemed to be invisible to those who were organizing events at the scene. I should have swiftly got myself away and back to my own beat, that was what an experienced officer would have done. I lingered and half an hour later I was one of the only officers still present.

The detective inspector had decided that a search of the scene could be better conducted in daylight and he told his officers to go home and report back in six hours. Uniformed officers began to disappear in all directions but I was too slow and the inspector told me to stay until he returned. I was to guard the area from interference for six hours.

Later, after I had been standing near the toilets for an hour or two, I heard control telling a concerned sergeant that I was "guarding a condom". For me guarding a crime scene was fine, I had been determined to do better than last time, but to be referred to as guarding a used durex was a step in the direction of embarrassing!

As I stood, sauntered and stamped in an effort to keep warm I got to thinking. I could not understand anyone wanting to have sex in the flower bed I was guarding. It was not a floral tribute to the local council, rather it was a collection of thistles, weeds and other spikey plants, no doubt fertilized by dog dirt and decaying litter. Nor could I imagine a rapist being so considerate as to struggle into a condom as he attacked his victim and if he had worn a condom to prevent forensic evidence being recovered then surely, he would not leave that evidence neatly wrapped at the crime scene.

I started sneezing about two hours before my shift should officially have finished, but I had been told to remain till the inspector came back. An hour after I should have gone off duty, I radioed in to ask if I was going to be relieved. I was now sweating and felt terrible. Control said they would check what was happening and I waited another hour. Eventually the message came. "Could you please collect the tape that surrounded the crime scene and return to the station immediately".

On arrival at the station, I was asked if the condom had passed a quiet night and other sarcastic comments. Worst of all though was the message recorded on the log of the incident. The woman had withdrawn her allegations minutes after I had been left to guard the scene. There was no condom to guard. The woman had wanted her boyfriend to walk her home and in true gentlemanly fashion he had refused. The rape allegation was to make him feel guilty for abandoning her. She had apologized for wasting police time and as she had been well drunk it was unlikely any action would be taken against her. No one apologized to me and I felt like I was dying!

Mrs Jennings had excelled herself, both sides of the breakfast were burned on this occasion, clearly the delay in my getting home had enabled her to perfect the technique. I could not cut anything let alone chew it and it was a relief when she realized I was ill. She had, she declared, a home-made miracle cure for fevers and colds. As I sat at the breakfast table, she poured about a quarter of a pint of hundred percent proof Polish Vodka into a glass; to this she added two table spoons of ground black pepper. I was instructed to drink this concoction in one swig. I did and immediately felt like my chest was on fire. I thought I was going to be sick and rushed upstairs to the bathroom and bed. I cannot then remember anything until I woke up near teatime. My uniform was strewn across the floor but worse, the sheets were soaked. I was convinced I had wet the bed and got up ready to apologise to Mrs Jennings. The reality was that I had sweated the fever out of my system, I felt well, though very thirsty....

The rest of the week of nights passed in a flash. On our first day off the entire shift got up early and went to watch a stripper in a local club. Nowadays I believe things are very different but then even the female constables came. As days became weeks, I realized that most of the officers socialized with no one away from the work environment. The shift was the centre of all activity, work, rest and play. These close-knit cliques often had incredible camaraderie and every member would go to the ends of the earth for any other member. Perhaps it was not healthy and looking back I do think it could have been a closed shop whose culture permitted wrongdoing as well as positive action. However, I did not have those thoughts at the time, and a strange mish mash of former postal workers, bank clerks, teachers, joiners etc quickly became part of my new Police family.

CHAPTER SIX

ONWARDS

In retrospect my first year as a Probationer Constable was a collection of experiences most of which were not very memorable. I think that that is probably the case for the majority of officers. After all, you are not allowed to patrol alone for the first few weeks of your service so everything you do is shared with someone else, you cannot drive the patrol cars until you have been tested and historically the detectives did most of the real crime work.

None of the statements I have just made can be said to be a hundred percent true. For example, I spent most of my time patrolling alone during my first week of nights and things vary from Force to Force and time to time. Basically, you do a bit of this and a bit of that and usually become totally proficient in nothing.

On my first day shift, patrolling without anyone to hold my hand, I was sent to the town museum where someone was causing a commotion. There on my arrival I saw two display cabinets with their glass fronts smashed. I could hear noise further in the building and on arriving in an archaeological section I saw two scruffy youths sword fighting in a display of a roman British settlement. I called for assistance because it was clear this had to stop and I was outnumbered. I cannot remember saying much to the youths but I was convinced I should arrest them. I cannot remember telling them what I was arresting them for and, to be honest, in the heat of the moment I did not know!

I grabbed one of the youths and was immediately struck by the other with a wooden sword. Further officers arrived and after a struggle the display resembled post eruption Pompei. At the station I entered the Charge Office from a different door than the prisoners. "What have we got here?" Asked the sergeant.

"He done us for smashing up the museum". Offered one of the youths.

"Is that correct?" The sergeant asked me.

I stuttered that it was correct and the sergeant got on with processing the youths. This process, something I would become very familiar with later in my career, involved identifying the prisoners, searching them, checking if they had criminal records and placing them in cells. As my prisoners, my very first prisoners, walked off the sergeant was looking at me carefully. He asked what they had done and what I thought they should be charged with.

I had been thinking about this and had recalled studying the offence of Criminal Damage at training school. The problem was I could not remember if there was a power of arrest for that offence. I had been hit by the wooden roman sword and knew it was an offence to assault a police officer but I could not remember if I had to have visible injuries for this. Then I latched on public order offences where the Queens Peace is disturbed by unruly behaviour. I was pretty certain the museum was a public place because you did not have to pay to go in.

From nowhere I blurted, "Breach of the Peace".

"Good Lad! That's what you arrested them for and now we will get statements, question them and report them for criminal damage."

In those days there was no Crown Prosecutions Service and the Police decided who would be prosecuted and what for. There was a Force Solicitors Office to provide advice in difficult cases and present those cases at court, but most cases were prepared by and presented in court by Police Officers.

I managed to cover myself in black ink while fingerprinting the youths. They apologized and I never raised the roman sword attack with the sergeant. Later both of them were Bound over to Keep the Peace, fined ten pounds for criminal damage and ordered to pay compensation to the museum.

That incident may not be particularly exciting and my prisoners were not major criminals, they were, however, my first prisoners and Probation was full of lots of little things like that. I found locking up drunks who were misbehaving a particularly easy way of keeping my sergeants happy. The offence of being Drunk and Disorderly seemed to be able to be stretched to cover almost any situation. For example, urinating in a shop doorway was something which really upset the keepers of those shops and their staff but there was no power of arrest for doing it. However, if you arrested the person for being drunk and disorderly, they were dealt with and often fined within days. I cannot remember anyone ever trying to say that they were not drunk, which always amazed me as that was the whole basis of the offence.

A Police Officer had to provide evidence that a person was drunk and he did this by using the same formula of words in every report, "I noticed that the accused was unsteady on his feet, his speech was slurred, his breath smelled of alcohol and he was drunk".

Most of those arrested clearly fitted all those criteria, however, there were exceptions. Sometimes the alleged 'drunk' would set off to run away before they were arrested and I have seen some spectacularly quick and agile drunks who were not so unsteady on their feet that they could not give fit police offices a good run for their money. I guess, in those days, individuals were happier to admit being drunk rather than have everyone know they urinated in public.

In the late 1970's and the early1980's standards of behaviour on a city street were far better than they seem to be now. We prosecuted people who used the 'F' word in a public place when women and children were about. People being reported for that offence often apologised for having been rude. Now on the same streets young women are often the worst offenders when it comes to bad language and it seems that there would be little communication without using obscenities as link words.

Whilst I found making arrests a painless way of doing my job, I was less successful at reporting people for traffic offences. On one day I returned to the police station for my refreshment break. As I let myself into the warm corridor and started to take off my jacket I was grabbed by the elbow.

"My Office, now!"

As I turned, I saw the back of one of the station's Chief Inspectors disappearing towards an office. I followed him, as I quickly tried putting my half off jacket back on again. Once inside there was no offer for me to sit down. Walt Wallace was an old-style police officer who had progressed steadily through the ranks after leaving the army. His short hair was Bryl creamed and brushed straight back from his forehead. He was a slim man who wore gold rimmed glasses through which he peered at you as if the lenses were not strong enough for him.

"How many ticks today then, lad?" He asked.

For a moment I was not certain what he meant and then recollected that I had heard Traffic Officers referring to "ticks" when they were totting up how many offences they had reported during a period of time.

"None today, Sir. Not yet. It's very quiet." I managed to stutter.

"Rubbish, lad. Rubbish. Where are you going now?"

"Refreshments, Sir."

"Cancel that then, you can eat when you've done some work. Come with me."

He got up from his desk, put a cream raincoat on over his uniform and told me to follow him. Out we went back onto the very street I had just left. There was a steady flow of vehicles and pedestrians but everything seemed fine and orderly to me. The Chief Inspector saw it differently and as a car pulled onto the pavement, he swept towards it as if radar directed.

"Approach the driver." He told me and as I did this, he hovered just behind me.

As I ascertained the driver's details my shadow kept prompting me.

"First offence driving on the footpath"

"Did you know it was an offence to drive a motor vehicle on the footpath?" I asked the driver.

"No," he replied "I just thought it would be safer to park here than on the road."

"Second offence, illegal parking." The Chief Inspector pointed out.

This went on for some time through a bald tyre, an out-of-date vehicle excise licence, a faulty brake light and an inoperative handbrake which became apparent when the driver got out of his car to find his driving licence. I issued the man with an HORT1 Form which required him to produce the driving licence, that he could not find, and his insurance at a police station. The car had hardly returned to the road when my mentor approached a shop where a sign standing on the footpath announced that the tobacconist sold ready rubbed tobacco. I was informed that it was a Bye Law Offence to obstruct the footpath with a 'sign, advertisement or hoarding'.

We remained on the street together for little over half an hour and when we returned to the station, we had only dealt with four people but I had twenty-six ticks in a morning. This I was told was just about "acceptable". It took me hours of paperwork to submit all the statements, documents and reports needed to secure summons and court appearances. For me the lesson was to dodge the Chief Inspector, for others and especially Traffic Officers this sort of supervision inspired a mad competition to secure the most "ticks".

I heard of one Traffic Officer, Peter Biglin who regularly submitted over a thousand 'ticks' in a month. On occasion it was claimed the magistrates asked him to ease off and when he did not, they held extra court sittings called "Biglin Courts" just to clear his backlog.

Though Walt Wallace caused me an enormous amount of work on that day he also saved me a bit of embarrassment on another occasion.

One evening I was walking back to the station and approaching the public gardens at the front of the building when I saw a man picking daffodils from a floral display. He had a large armful of flowers and as I approached, he threw them down and ran. I chased him, running as fast as I could in a tunic and Ganex raincoat. Eventually, I tried my old fall back, a rugby tackle. I caught the man's ankle as I reached full stretch and from a position on the floor, I saw him take off, hit the ground, bounce once and end up in an ornamental pond covered in pond weed. I 'rescued' him and dragged him across the gardens to the station. Along the way he told me he had forgotten his mother's birthday and that he was a soldier on leave. I wanted to let him go but the dramatic enactment had caused quite a bit of attention.

In the Charge Office the sergeant asked the reason for arrest as he looked disapprovingly at the water and weed collecting on his office floor.

"Theft of Daffodils," I said.

The sergeant said nothing, his face started to go a deep reddish colour and he seemed to be holding something back. Something like a none too minor volcanic eruption! It was at this stage that I noticed Walt Wallace typing at a table behind the sergeant.

"I think PC Marchbank means to say that he has arrested this man for Drunk and Disorderly while the fellow was behaving riotously among the flowers. Isn't that right officer?"

"Yes, Sir" I hastily replied.

"Thank God for that." Interjected my prisoner.

Walt was less than impressed by this,

"There is no need to blaspheme young man. I am sure we can find other charges for you."

My prisoner looked sullenly at the floor and then winked at me. After he was processed, I escorted him to a drunk cell (the same as any other cell, but the bed was only six inches off the ground). He seemed to have recovered his composure.

"They'll come for me within an hour or two. Theft could have got me in real bother, this will just be a discipline job. Thanks for not pushing it with the theft. Have you got any magazines?"

I had no idea what he was talking about until I returned to the Charge Office where the sergeant was on the telephone. Walt Wallace smiled up at me from the desk.

"Not your finest hour Marchbank. The man was obviously a 'squaddie', there are all sorts of jurisdiction problems with there being a barracks just up the road. They'll come and collect your chap and deal with him themselves. Theft would have been a bit strong for a few flowers, he'd have served time in the military cells and possibly lost his job. Now everyone is fairly happy. Do a short report for the soldiers who pick him up."

I left the office relieved that everyone did indeed seem to be happy. I felt relieved that again I had got away with leaping in on something and lacking the experience to see more than one outcome. I often wondered if Policing was all about luck and, on retrospection, I remain convinced that a lot of it is!

After being a police officer for nearly six months I received a letter signed by the Chief Constable. It told me that I had been selected for the next stage of the Accelerated Promotion Scheme. This involved a series of interviews and tests at the Derbyshire Police Headquarters. I had to make my own way there, accommodation and food would be provided and plainclothes would be worn.

I had no idea what would take place but it would mean I missed three shifts on my week of "Nights". This was good news and I did not give anything else much thought. My father drove me to Derbyshire and I was to catch a train back two days later. From arrival to departure the process was intimidating!

There were about sixty candidates present and on the first evening we gathered in the Bar of the Headquarters building. After a short time, it became clear that many of those in the Bar were in fact Chief Officers from a variety of Forces, my own Chief Constable entered the room a little before closing time. Some of the candidates seemed to be on familiar terms with some of the Chief Officers. I was not even certain if my Chief Constable would recognize me when I was out of uniform.

After breakfast the following day we were all gathered in a large room, given instructions and timings for the next two days. I started off with two half hour interviews, then something called a 'Group Exercise", in the afternoon I had a 'Group Discussion". The following day involved a general knowledge test, a numeracy test, a problem-solving test and a psychological evaluation.

The first interview went quite well. In 1978 most people were wearing stacked heel shoes. My shoes were stacked but that was not really evident as my slightly flared suit trousers covered all but the lower part of the footwear. As I stood in front of the interview panel, I was probably an assisted six feet three inches tall. My hair was short, as was that of most probationary constables and I was fairly fit through a lot of sport.

"Are you a Guardsman?" Asked one of my interview panel.

"No, Sir."

"You look like one. Very smart, a credit!"

The others sat nodding and the questions they asked did not seem too tasking. It was obvious that this panel were all Chief Officers, though few of their questions were directly related to police duties. As I left the room, I felt the interview had gone quite well but to this day I cannot remember the questions.

The second interview was not as friendly an experience. This panel were Home Office Civil Servants and I must admit I had no idea what they were talking about most of the time. I answered their questions, never froze, but there was no indication of whether or not I was saying anything valid or totally idiotic.

The Group Discussion was one of the worst experiences of my life. I had never come across anything like it. As soon as the subject to be discussed was read out some of my group were spurting out statements as if they had prepared in advance, it was impossible to get a word in, then one 'helpful soul' asked me what I thought, as if to emphasise I had said nothing. I did eventually manage a bit of summing up just before time was called. However, my overwhelming desire as we left the room was to beat the living daylights out of one or two of the group. I believed that most of those present had behaved in a bumptious, pretentious manner and often spoke without thinking first. I detested them and the thought of continuing this painful process in their presence was almost too traumatic to think about.

I rang my father and asked if he would come and get me. I told him what had happened and waited for the sympathy that never really came. The message was to get on with it. The situation, he felt, would be as bad for everyone else and tomorrow was another day. I had to stop!

The tests were not too bad but I had no idea what the psychological stuff was all about. Then it was all over and we were directed to the dining room for lunch. It was at this stage that I am convinced luck took a hand. I sat down at my table after most people had already taken their places. The main course was Plaice and New Potatoes with Vegetables. On the tables were silver plated bowls which contained an almost grey cream sauce. I asked one of the catering staff what sort of sauce it was and she looked at me as if I had just arrived from outer space.

"Tartare". She grunted and walked on.

Well, I sniffed the sauce and put a little on the edge of my fork and tasted it. It was certainly not tartare sauce. I was pretty certain it was, in fact, horse radish sauce and I was about to get on with my meal when I thought, "No" I will go and ask for some proper sauce. So, I picked up the bowl and walked towards the swing door to the kitchens, realizing as I did so that I was being watched by the Chief Officers and Civil Servants on the top table. In the kitchen I explained why I was there.

The reaction was initially disbelief, then realisation and then unexpected action. A large black lady picked up a huge catering size jar of tartare sauce and a spoon. She gave me a dozen or so empty bowls and then said,

"You come with me."

We marched back into the dining room and as I put a bowl on each table, she dolloped a large spoonful of sauce into it. Most of those present had by now almost completed eating. All of those who had had sauce had eaten horseradish with plaice without any question. I explained what was going on to one of the Chief Officers as the kitchen assistant emptied her jar at his table. I saw him telling his neighbour and shortly almost all the top table were smiling or laughing.

Two weeks later I got a letter telling me I had been successful at the Extended Interview and offering me a place on the Special Course at the Police Staff College, Bramshill. To this day I am convinced that I got through because I knew the difference between tartare and horseradish! If that is the case then luck certainly was smiling on me.

Nowadays the Police use Extended Interviews for promotion to almost all ranks. Usually, the process is run and at the end of the process a pass mark is set. Those who achieve that mark are then eligible for promotion as vacancies occur. Some say that this is fairer more efficient than relying on favouritism, nepotism or gut reaction but I have my doubts.

The process and the type of tests are now well known. Officers spend hours and hours working on their techniques and treat it all as a game. Some people who are absolutely useless as police officers are world beaters at assessment centres (where the extended interview format is used). I had a superintendent working for me at one time who started to disappear for large chunks of the day. I found him going over and over psychometric tests so that his answers would match certain character traits.

The result is, in my opinion, that the Police, along with other organisations, operate a system that delivers them average clones as its end product. You can watch officers appearing before cameras or at meetings and their answers are exactly what they would say in an exercise. The result is often that you get format rather than feeling, and safety rather than risk. I guess it's the world we live in.

Anyway, to return to the real world, or the world of 1978. I was still enjoying walking my various beats and finding new things to do. Every now and then a patrol car driver would pick me up and drive me around their area for an hour or so. This was not supposed to happen and the sergeants frowned on it but it did give you a chance to see the world of policing from a different, more relaxed angle. I enjoyed walking but eight hours was a long time to be on your feet and you needed to be fit to do it day in and day out.

Some officers detested walking and I became aware that many of them abused the 'tea spots' which we all knew about and used. Tea spots came in all shapes and sizes but were places where officers knew they could go and get warm, sit down and usually be offered some form of refreshment. I had a tea spot on my usual beat in the kitchens of a Chinese restaurant where you could sit next to the chefs, keep warm on the coldest of days and often be given samples of what was being cooked. My friend on a neighbouring beat used to be allowed into the projectionist's room at a local picture house and there he would sit, sometimes through a full film, drinking tea and resting his feet on another chair.

A strange way of dodging foot patrol was practised by an officer called Danny Asquith. Danny's father had, like mine, been an officer before him and great things had been expected of young Danny. Unfortunately, he was not the brightest of individuals, he found it difficult to talk to people, paperwork was a continual problem and he hated walking a beat. Because he struggled with the basics no one pushed him forward for the driving course which was necessary before you were qualified to drive police vehicles.

Danny was like a ticking time bomb. He knew how much was expected of him, he also knew he was underachieving but he blamed that on not being able to drive police cars and he decided on two new tactics to solve his problems. When booking off duty officers used to have to hand their radios in so that their batteries could be recharged and then re allocated to other officers. Danny decided to 'acquire' a radio and take it home with him. This meant that even when he was off duty, he knew what was going on. The next step was more controversial because he would turn up when off duty and try to get to potentially exciting jobs before the officers who were despatched. He managed to get in the way at several incidents and was beginning to annoy his colleagues.

One day, as I walked towards the scene of an alleged disturbance, I was narrowly missed by a Morris minor car which was travelling at speed, the wrong way down a one-way street. When I got to the incident Danny was there already as was the Morris Minor and a long-haired youth was lying on the floor.

"I've got this one," shouted Danny, "the others ran off down there." He pointed down a narrow alley.

I asked what had been going on and was told that three or four youths had been fighting. There was now no fight, the street was quiet so I decided to help Danny with his prisoner.

"Whose car, is it?" I asked.

He told me that it was his as he dragged the youth up from the ground and pushed him on all fours into the back of the Morris. We then travelled most of the way back to the station in the car before Danny stopped about four hundred meters from our destination. Then he switched off the engine and asked me

64

to help him escort the prisoner to the Charge Office. I did this and then resumed patrol. Something had not been right with what I had just seen happen. Danny was in full uniform and had made an arrest, he had a radio and so appeared to be on duty. Yet in spite of this he had been in his own car which he had driven illegally. The whole story was soon to be made known to me.

Danny was supposed to be having a day off. He had, however, decided to patrol in his own car and show what he could do. He heard about the disturbance and got there as fast as he could, using his car as if it were a patrol car. On arrival at the fight, he had driven straight in to the middle of it and his prisoner had been knocked to the ground by impact with the Morris. The prisoner had recovered but was considering making a complaint against Police. The inspector had tried to tell Danny how stupid he had been and Danny responded by blaming the inspector for not having got him a driving course. The two had to be dragged apart and Danny was sent home.

He was interviewed by what is today called Professional Standards but which then was the Discipline and Complaints Department and, as he was still a probationary constable, his services were dispensed with. I saw him, from a distance, on the day he learned his fate. He was kicking his helmet along a corridor in the police station and shouting abuse into any office that had an open door. It all seemed very sad because all he had wanted to do was be a success, he was misguided but not a bad person. This at least was what I thought at the time. He went on to become a real pain for serving officers. He still turned up at jobs, usually having been drinking and would hurl abuse at officers trying to perform their duties.

Eventually he was arrested for drunk driving and at court claimed he had been set up because he knew how corrupt the police were. The magistrates did not believe him and he continued to be a problem until marriage and the arrival of children enabled him to find his balance again.

If Danny felt the pressure to succeed because of his father, then I certainly did not share that with him. However, my father was one of the reasons why I still could not drive at twenty-six years of age. My mother still says that I had no interest in driving and she may be right, to an extent. Why would you want to drive if you had no chance of ever having a car? The car in our family was my father's exclusive domain. He was a good driver and, though I have no idea why you would want to, he could drive with a full glass of water on the dashboard and not spill any!

When I was coming up to university/leaving home he was driving an Alvis which had been a doctor's car, though it looked like something Al Capone would have used. It had running boards along each side that you could stand on and the interior was real wood and leather. I remember going on a family holiday to Scotland in it. My brother and I stood on the back seat and waved out of the sunroof at any pedestrians we passed, but if that was a good memory there were plenty of bad ones. The exhaust had a hole in it and at time the air in the back turned blue, worse than that though was the occasion we visited relatives and I put my foot through the running board when getting out. As I stood there trapped and manacled by the car my father and a male relative discussed the best way to do the repair. Everyone then went inside the house and I was left with the vehicle imprisoning me until an afterthought caused someone to come and get me.

My father taught several friend's children to drive, he was after all a former police traffic driver and the Road Safety Officer. He was, apparently, patient, helpful and informative with all his pupils……at least when they were not family members. My mother had a job at a driving school as an office manager and receptionist, the company taught her to drive and she passed her test at the first go with no help from my father. She then expected to be able to drive the family car but after being shouted at by my father on the first time she changed gear she never ever drove again in the UK.

The driving school provided me with reduced price lessons but I was not good at it. Only slowly did I get a grip of the language. The instructor, a large man called Peter, would say "Gas, Gas, more Gas" and all I could think of were exhaust fumes. It was the third lesson before I fully realized that he meant I should accelerate. My father never offered to supplement the lessons by taking me out with him. Perhaps he knew it would not work. If so, he should have stuck to his guns because when I had to attend an interview at a university, he said he would borrow a car and I could drive.

The whole journey was a disaster and as I went to make a tight left-hand turn, I crossed over the central white line. Nothing was coming the other way but you would have thought I had just sunk the Titanic. He grabbed the steering wheel and pulled it to the left just as I accelerated to complete the turn. We clipped the kerb and mounted the pavement. Horns were blaring from vehicles behind us and pedestrians were looking worried. After we had stopped there was a lot of huffing and puffing and technical car speak, then I was told to sit in the back and get ready for the interview.

Like my mother, I had no urge to drive again, though I did make a hundred-mile round trip on a moped once. Even that ended badly when I was almost back where I set out from. My hands were frozen and as a women pushed a pram in front of me, I could not squeeze the handbrake and ended up in a water filled ditch. That was definitely it, until one day in that first year with the police they told me I had got a driving course. I was not excited, I was quite happy walking, but it was obligatory.

The Force had its' own driving school and specially equipped dual control cars. There were some civilian driving instructors and a number of uniformed constables who also performed the role. Each car had an instructor and three pupils who took it in turn to drive. The idea was that you learned from what you saw others do as well as from what you did personally. There were a number of things that were done very differently at police driving training schools. Firstly, there was a 'Police System' that had to be followed, it was something like, COURSE, SPEED FOR COURSE, GEAR, INDICATE, MANOUEVRE as you drove you had to provide a commentary of what you were doing, for example, "I am driving in a straight line, road and weather conditions are good, traffic flow is light. I am following another vehicle. Ahead, I intend to turn left. I am reducing my speed for the turning; I have selected the appropriate gear and am indicating to turn."

The cars were usually Ford Escorts or sometimes Fiestas. There was much crunching of gears, a lot of swearing and quite a bit of shouting. I got so that I quite enjoyed driving on 'out of town' roads but the sweaty hands came back as soon as we re-entered built up areas. One girl in the car to which I was assigned made things a lot easier for me. She was useless, far, far worse than me and I would not have thought that possible. The driving instructor, a former army man, tried his best to be patient but every now and then expletives would burst forth and we had to stop while the female officer overcame an outburst of tears. I am not being sexist here, it just happened like that until one day the air became quite blue after we narrowly missed hitting a milk float. The girl stopped the car, threw the driver's door open and got out. The car rolled forward, engine in neutral, until the instructor stopped it and applied the handbrake. By the time we were safe the girl was gone, she was nowhere to be seen.

We drove round and round without being able to find her and time was passing. At last, the instructor stopped at a phone box and rang the sergeant in charge of the driving school. The instruction was to stay exactly where we were for an hour and then come back to base. The instructor was obviously worried and as he said there was now no good outcome. The female officer would be spoken to, she had absented herself from duty. However, she was bound to say that the instructor had sworn at her and did it regularly. He would be seen as having failed to maintain control.

As we drove back towards Headquarters we passed her walking along briskly, she had covered four or five miles. The instructor stopped, she got in and we drove off. Later the whole incident ended tamely. The girl was transferred to a different instructor and we carried on with only two pupils in the car. There was less swearing and a sleepy sort of atmosphere prevailed.

If the extra driving time in a two-pupil car had made me a better driver it did not show on the day of the test.

The driving school did its own testing and a sergeant took the passenger seat as I drove out of the station yard. It began well, my commentary seemed to be flowing, I managed the emergency stop perfectly and we moved away from the city centre to the roads where I was usually happy. Then, as we negotiated a roundabout near a large industrial site, the examiner asked me to take the turning at "eleven o' clock". I started to talk about that manoeuvre in my commentary and suddenly I realized I was way passed where that turning should have been.

"There is no turning at eleven o'clock." I announced.

"Oh! Yes, there is." Said the examiner. "Take the eleven o'clock turning when we come to it."

I was now totally confused because we were in a different place than when the first instruction had been given. I took the next turning, straight into the delivery area of a small factory. I had to reverse out onto the roundabout and that was the end of my first driving test. Failed! I remain adamant to this day that there was no turning at eleven o' clock but my views did not matter. Further, the examiner was clearly unimpressed with the overall quality of my driving as it was decided that I could not take the test again until I had repeated the entire course.

This failure to acquire my driving licence became an issue in a way I had not expected. It had seemed that everyone was happy with me walking the beat prior to the test but suddenly the same people were saying that it was time I did something different. I was initially sent on an attachment to the Traffic Division to see how that functioned, then I was posted to the Plainclothes section at my own station before finally ending up in the Custody Office in what was called Warder Duties. It was to be a frenetic time!

My time in Traffic was a restful interlude mainly spent dozing in the passenger seat of a three litre Ford Granada. I cannot even remember attending a traffic accident (now called "collisions"). What I do remember is sitting in a line of five traffic cars, the entire night time cover for the whole Force, waiting to judge the shortest skirt as girls left the Trocadero Club. I also remember a very embarrassing experience during the hours of daylight.

Philip Biglin, the officer who had been a scourge of the magistrate's courts as a constable, had now risen to the heights of inspector. In those days all inspectors were regarded as the next thing down from God. Specialist inspectors such as those in Traffic and the CID were held in even higher esteem and Biglin was a legend amongst giants. The most experienced traffic officers were in awe in his presence, he was a large man with a cutting and sarcastic manner. He had done it all!

My driver and I were parked at the end of a narrow country lane on a sunny but cold winters day. We were waiting for a visit from Inspector Biglin and the traffic man was busy making sure his notebook was up to date. I was nervous beyond reason and trying to think what he might ask me and how I should answer. Eventually a second Granada pulled up in front of ours and a large, square bodied, grizzled man got out and made his way towards us. For some reason I leapt out of the car and started trying to put down the back of my seat. My intention was to get in the back of the car so that the inspector could have the front seat.

I struggled with levers, pushed and pulled and puffed and panted.

"What the Fuck are you doing?" Boomed the voice from the man behind me.

I explained quickly and continued to tug and pull at the seat.

"If you get out of the Fucking way, I will open the back door!"

I suddenly realized that my nerves had made a fool of me. I was used to two door Fiestas and Escorts and the Granada was a large four door saloon. All I had to do was get out open the back door and get in the back seat.

"Where did you get this Clown?" Biglin asked my driver.

Then without waiting for a reply he launched into a tirade against Chief Officers, politicians and the general public. Having worked himself into a frenzy he started to focus in on his audience. How many offences had we reported today? What accident blackspots had we visited? Were our notebooks up to date? How had I managed to get in the Police when I was obviously thick as "bloody pig shit"?

Then he got out of our car, walked round it and looked at all four tyres and then went back to his own vehicle and drove off. That was my first meeting with a legend. I did not feel inspired, enthused or ready to pledge my life to the Traffic Division. I just felt monumentally embarrassed and wished the ground would open up and suck me in. I still felt like that even when my colleague told me that Biglin had the same effect on everyone.

If Inspector Biglin created my first embarrassing moment in the Police, then the second was all my own doing. I mention it now because it relates to cars and driving. I eventually passed my driving test at the second attempt at a time when I was working in the Custody Office. Immediately upon getting my licence my attitude to driving changed. I wanted to drive. I wanted a car of my own and I was convinced that I was now a good driver.

One night a drunk driver was brought into the custody office and a doctor was called, asking him to come to the station and take a sample of blood from the alleged offender. When the doctor arrived in the Custody Office, he seemed considerably worse for drink than the driver had been. I opened the surgery and the doctor managed to lay out his equipment and put on a pair of rubber gloves, the prisoner was then brought in. As the doctor swayed backwards and forwards the prisoner turned ashen and after several attempts to find a vein, I thought he might faint. Eventually a sample was obtained and the prisoner, no doubt feeling like a pin cushion, was returned to his cell.

The doctor, who must have frightened himself, did the decent thing and asked if someone could give him a lift home. I immediately volunteered and to my amazement was told to go and get a car. This was to be my first solo drive and the nerves started to kick in. The doctor got in the passenger seat and I started the car and lifted the clutch to move off. We then shot backwards and collided with one of the petrol pumps in the station yard. I put the car in neutral and got out to view what had happened and as there did not appear to be any damage I drove the doctor home.

When I returned to the station the yard was sealed off and a fire engine was positioned near to the petrol pumps. I parked and went back to the Custody Office where the sergeant was extremely agitated.

"Trying to blow us all up, were you?" He asked

I looked at him blankly, though I was beginning to realize what must have happened.

"When did you pass your test?"

I told him and he threw his hands up in the air before flopping down into his seat at the office desk.

After I had left someone had noticed a strong smell of petrol near the pumps. There had also been a pool of liquid at the base of the pump. The Fire Service had been called and the liquid turned out not to be petrol but rain water that had collected in the upper works of the pump casing. Someone had spilled petrol at one of the other pumps so I was not to blame. However, the recording from the security camera in the yard did show my car leap back at the pump and make contact. A disaster had only narrowly been avoided and it was a long time before people let me forget.

It was not long after the petrol pump attacked my car that I was posted, on attachment, to the Plainclothes Section. We were really a little Vice Squad, focusing on prostitution, pornography, licensing and a multitude of other jobs where it helped not to be in uniform. It was a good job and one that I would have been happy to spend a lot longer at. However, my first experience made me realize that there were advantages to being in uniform.

There had been serious rioting in London and one or two other cities across the UK. In many areas nothing major took place but there was a continuous fear that copycat disturbances might take place. This did in fact happen in the Division to which I was attached. Four of us from the Plainclothes Section had been sent to visit pubs in the city to see if anyone was trying to stir up trouble. We saw nothing but publicans expressed a feeling that something was indeed bubbling just beneath the surface.

About ten o' clock in the evening stones were thrown at a police van on one of the main streets in the city centre. We were sent to find out where the attackers had gone to and how many of them there were.

In a pub situated at the side of the bus station we found a large group of very agitated young people. Some of them were recognizable as belonging to the troublesome element of the local football team. I could see no sign of any weapons and very few of them were drinking, it seemed as if they were waiting for something to happen. Then, all of a sudden, the whole group surged towards the door of the pub and out into the bus station. We waited briefly, informed our control what was happening and then followed them.

By the time we caught up there were about fifty or sixty of them making their way across a piece of open land that the Council used as a carpark. A Police Transit Van was driving along a road at the side of the land and after an interval of shouting, chanting and abuse the youths began running towards it. They picked up rubble from the floor of the car park and hurled it in the general direction of the van which to my surprise stopped. The stationary target now started to receive a bombardment of stones, bottles and pieces of metal. Although no longer running the attackers were still making their way towards the van.

As I watched, not certain quite what to do to help, the doors of the van opened. Five or six police officers climbed out. It seemed to me to be total idiocy to deploy such a small group against so many disorderly youths. I saw a shape run towards the police officers, he had a scarf wrapped round the lower part of his face and he was carrying a beer bottle. Almost robotically I found myself running towards this figure and as he drew his arm back to throw the bottle I did it again. I rugby tackled him just below his knees and both of us hit the floor with a crunch.

The scarf had come away from the face of the youth I had brought down and as I tried to get up without letting go of him, he tried to bite me. We were now struggling on the ground but everything seemed to be in slow motion. None of the other youths in the group seemed to be interfering in our tussle and in the distance, I could see more police vans arriving. Briefly a full-scale street fight was taking place between the stone throwers and the police; then I saw a police officer running towards my position. I had an immense feeling of relief until I saw him raise his truncheon.

I came round in the city hospital with a large egg-shaped lump on the side of my head and I quickly found I could not straighten my right arm. The curtained cubicles on either side of where I was receiving treatment were full of injured police officers and their would-be attackers. A nurse told me to lay still and stay in my cubicle. I did not feel too bad but did as I was told, after all it was warm and seemed safe and I was still being paid!

I was discharged the following morning after I proved I could count how many fingers a doctor had and I made my way home on foot with my head bandaged and my arm in a sling. The following day I woke about lunchtime and realised that I would have to pull myself together to get to work in time. I should have taken the day off sick and it sounds macho as I write this now, but all I wanted to do was get to work and discuss the previous nights' events. Within an hour of getting to work I wished I had stopped in bed.

The youth whom I had tackled and held on to had been arrested but he had complained of assault. He was saying I attacked him for no reason and that I was one of the people throwing stones at the police van. He also claimed that he had been assaulted by a second officer who had hit him with a truncheon. The Discipline and Complaints Department wanted my notebook, meanwhile my sergeant wanted a full report based on what was in that notebook. The problem was that I did not know where the book was! It had been in my jeans when I went out to observe potential rioters but I did not have it now and consequently wherever it was it was out of date.

Over the coming hours everyone seemed to want to talk to me. The constable who I had seen running towards me wanted my assurance that I would say I did not see him using his truncheon. He was not pleased when I pointed out that his truncheon had most likely caused all my injuries. The press wanted to talk to officers who had been present at the "battle" but we were not allowed to as it could jeopardise the coming court case. Most worryingly Discipline and Complaints would not leave me alone.

I eventually found my notebook at the hospital and explained, to those who asked, that I had made it up to date at the first possible opportunity. The complete absence of any details after my tackling the youth was due to the fact that I was out cold. At court I did say I could not recall seeing the officer who struck me using a truncheon but then my" prisoner" was also found not guilty of assaulting me. Most of those arrested at the "battle" were charged with relatively minor public order offences, the serious offences of riot or affray were not used. Ironically, I think it is because we nipped the developing situation in the bud that many of the arrested never went on to find themselves facing serious prison sentences. I thought that was a success but some would have disagreed.

CHAPTER SEVEN

DEATH IN ALL ITS' FORMS

All police officers have to face up to death. Many face life threatening scenarios during their careers, others end up investigating murders but all of them end up dealing with 'sudden deaths'.

'Sudden deaths' are just that. Someone has died but no one is quite certain why they died. A doctor will pronounce life extinct but sometimes they will not issue a death certificate that will set out the cause of death. The doctor may not have seen the patient for a long period of time or genuinely cannot find or speculate on a cause of death. The great majority of such deaths have no suspicious circumstances but the police are called to all of them.

I had only been a police officer for a few months when I was sent to my first 'death'. I am sure that every officer, past or present, will remember their first such event. Those who remain constables for their entire career will deal with hundreds of deaths. In doing so they develop a hard crust that protects them from the emotion that always accompanies such events. The great majority rely on black humour, stories and jokes that help desensitize them as they approach the next death.

For me, my first death came as a shock. It was not the shock of death itself or the gruesome circumstances, it was simply the fact that I felt absolutely nothing. I had feared that emotion would prevent me dealing with the administrative procedures and somehow let down the deceased and their family and yet the reality was that I wondered if I was even a human being.

My first death was a male, about five feet six inches tall, stoutly built with thinning hair and he was in his early sixties. He lived alone in the flat where a neighbour had found him. A doctor had been called and he had pronounced life extinct but had not felt able to issue a death certificate. As a result, I accompanied the deceased to the city mortuary. I helped undress the body and then placed his clothing in a property bag. He was given an identifying number and placed in a body fridge.

I had not wobbled, sobbed, forgotten procedure or felt anything different than I would, say, cleaning the car. Surely, I should have felt something? The Coroners' Officer clearly did not feel any empathy with the deceased, he kept his sandwiches, pork pies and milk in the fridge with the bodies. I wanted to feel something but all I had was a feeling of numbness.

A little later my sergeant arrived with the man's son. I retrieved the body from the fridge for the son to see and identify his father. As I did so the sergeant told me that father and son had been playing snooker together an hour before the neighbour found the man dead in his flat. As I prepared the body for viewing, I noticed that the man had blue snooker chalk on his fingers. Suddenly something snapped. I now did feel the sadness and emotion. The fact of a father and son enjoying a game before a life had been snuffed out triggered a wave of empathy within me. I felt human again. The death became a personal tragedy and not just a business transaction.

I was relieved to feel human after all, the sentimental streak was still there. I wanted to put my arm around the man's son and give him a hug but instead I was frozen by a combination of macho behaviour and being a police officer.

When I thought about the experience afterwards it seemed to me that dealing with death involved either being detached and professional or emotionally involved and absolutely useless. As I dealt with more deaths I decided being detached and yet supportive was the best approach for the relatives of the deceased; they after all were, in the modern parlance, 'the customer' and they needed someone to rely on not just a body to share their grief.

Many police officers who have just returned from training school are subjected to the 'mortuary initiation'. The usual format would be to send the new officer to see Mr. Burnham at the mortuary. There a colleague would be lying under a sheet on a 'body trolley' and as the rookie would enter a slightly darkened room the colleague would sit up with a wailing noise. You can imagine the shocked state of those who had no inkling of what was going to happen.

There was nothing to like about visiting the mortuary. For me the smell was the worst thing. It was not the expected smell of decaying bodies but rather the air fresheners that were used. It was a vile cloying smell that clung to your uniform for days after every visit. I recall that this stuff came in silver foil and when unwrapped they resembled large green wax candles. These were inserted in the air conditioning system so that there was no escaping from the smell.

Looking back on my first 'sudden death', with the benefit of hindsight, I believe that my response was triggered by shock rather than professional detachment. Years later I witnessed the effect of shock on the wife of a deceased. Her husband had been working on an oil rig when a hawser had snapped under immense pressure. His body was literally cut in two with one half being swept into the sea and never recovered. I had to take the 'death message' to the wife.

I did all the things that we were trained to do. I brought a friend in, made us all a cup of tea, stressed that he would never have felt a thing and exactly what had happened. I offered to stay as long as she liked and volunteered to come back the following day if she wanted me to.

The lady seemed to calm down and steady herself and as I prepared to leave, she said,

"Please come tomorrow because my husband will be back by then and you should tell him."

This was a case of total shock where the bereaved's conscious had switched off in order to protect her nervous system. It was days before she came out of the trance like state and when she did, she broke down completely.

I was also involved in one incident where the state of shock may have impacted on me as well as the family of a deceased. It had been a pleasant spring day and I had parked next to a slowly flowing river where I was watching a number of swans gliding across the brown and muddy water. They seemed out of place set against the murky sludge they enhanced. Suddenly my radio burst into life.

I was despatched to a nearby village where a death had occurred at the cobbler's shop. The premises were difficult to find. The shop was the only one in the village and it transpired to be a ramshackle erection attached to a pristine white washed cottage.

In the doorway of the cottage stood a fleshy lady with rosy cheeks. She was wearing a floral-patterned dress with a cream apron over it. I approached her and with a beaming smile on her face she greeted me like a long-lost member of the family.

"Come in love," she said. "Come in and have a cup of tea. John and James are waiting for you."

I followed her into the low, dark living room of the cottage. There was a fire blazing in the hearth in spite of the warmth of the day outside. Two men were sat facing the fire, one in an armchair, the other at one end of a leather sofa.

"Sit you down." The lady invited. "Do you like sugar in your tea?"

I sat at the empty end of the sofa and she chattered away before approaching the three of us with cups of tea and a plate of biscuits. The cups were placed on both arms of the sofa and at the side of the chair. We then all sat together like a family gathering. The conversation ranged from the local football team to the speed of passing cars and the uselessness of the local Parish Council. I could have been there all day had not the radio controller tried to send me to another job.

"Well," I paused, "I suppose I ought to see the deceased."

The lady looked at me in surprise.

"You've been sat next to John for the last hour or more," she said with a smile on her face.

Imagine my feeling. I wished the earth could open up and swallow me. I knew for certain that I had spoken to the man sat next to me on the sofa and I knew the lady had given him a cup of tea and biscuit. From the initial shock I managed to regain my composure and behave in a professional manner, indeed I still visited the lady until I was moved to another Division.

The worst sudden death I ever attended was an old man who had died alone in his flat. It was some weeks before the neighbours were alerted by the smell and rang the Police. The deceased had been sat next to an electric fire and one of his legs had, in reality, cooked. The body burst when the undertakers tried to move it and the oil like liquid sprayed everywhere...

On another occasion an assistant bank manager failed to turn up to open the branch he worked at. He had died over night and was found in his bed as if he were asleep. The undertakers came and tried to prepare the body to take it to the mortuary. It soon became evident that this would not be easy as the man was huge, he was immensely fat and had a distended gut. Only after two hours effort did they get him into a temporary coffin. They struggled with the coffin towards the stairs and as they began to descend the deceased's' girlfriend arrived.

She literally threw herself onto the coffin shrieking hysterically. As a result, the bottom of the coffin fell out, followed by the body which slid down the stairs carrying the lower undertaker and the girlfriend with it. All three ended in an entangled heap at the bottom of the flight of stairs and it is amazing that neither of the living bodies were seriously injured by the fall.

Many years later, as a sergeant, I accompanied a probationer constable to the mortuary. We had been told that a body was being brought from another area. This was not unusual, especially where a neighbouring mortuary had been closed for refurbishment or had no spare space.

In this instance the body had been found in the nets of a fishing boat and was being conveyed by a single female undertaker. I tried to prepare the constable for the shock that a corpse recovered from the sea would usually provide. Further, I wondered about the experience of the undertaker and whether or not she had seen the sights that would await us.

The constable showed no signs of nerves or apprehension, indeed he also seemed concerned about the young woman accompanying the supposed sea ravaged body.

After a short time waiting in the mortuary, we heard a vehicle pulling up in the yard at the rear of the mortuary. I pressed the large red button that operated the shutters that formed the entry to the premises. The rattling and whirring noise broke the peace of the night and a green transit van now reversed up to the entrance.

The undertaker did not fit my stereotype. She was petite with an auburn bun and she was almost angelically pretty. The circumstances were not really a suitable setting for taking much note of those facts and heaving the body out of the van and onto the waiting gurney took all our effort and attention.

Once we were well inside the mortuary reception area, I unzipped the body bag and stepped back aghast at what I had seen. The body was largely decomposed and little flesh remained on the skull while the rest of the body was encased in oilskins and boots. The only thing to do was to 'pour' the body out of the bag and onto the metal gurney. This was accomplished with relative ease but as we did so a number of flat fish fell from the bag and continued flapping when they hit the floor.

"I've brought you a fry from Rotsea." Said the undertaker. (A 'fry' was a local way of saying some fish for you to cook…by frying.)

As she said that the constable fainted and collapsed on the floor in a heap among the gasping fish. He remained there while my stomach turned somersaults as the undertaker and I undressed what remained of the body and bagged the clothing.

Having completed the process, the young lady drove off into the night while I helped the constable recover from his ordeal. He declined a trip to hospital or a visit by the police surgeon and whenever I saw him, in the days to come, it was a subject he had no desire to discuss.

Suicides by gun, by hanging, by gassing. Suicides by drowning, poisoning and 'pact'. Suicide by bus, by train by police, by jumping off buildings. The number of varieties were almost endless but each resulted in a dead body that the police had to deal with.

I have come full circle. Police officers have to find a way of dealing with all that death and its variations in their daily work. In my early days as a police officer there was no 'stress counselling', I am amazed that we managed to remain sane, or largely sane most of the time.

CHAPTER EIGHT

ROWAN

You will notice that most of the characters that I share with you in these pages are colleagues from different stages of my career. Many of those I arrested or dealt with never became well known to me, I met them once and then never saw them again. However, there was one character who I bumped into several times and I possibly saved his life along the way.

I first met Rowan Martin in my early days as a constable. He was known to almost everyone and yet very few knew where he came from or how he came to lead the life that he did. Nowadays he would be described as a 'rough sleeper' but in the 1970's he was known as a 'tramp' or, perhaps more graphically, a 'plonky'. He would sit all day long on a park bench and his companion would almost always be a bottle of cheap cider.

He was a short man with a pinched face and a red nose. His hair was greying at his temples but you could see little else of his features. He wore a tweed flat cap pulled down onto his ears and a large, dirty, army greatcoat with the collar turned up and concealing most of his face. His legs were covered by baggy trousers and the picture was competed by a pair of scuffed boots that seemed several sizes too large for a man his size.

In winter Rowan would reside in the William Booth Hostel and if his behaviour there got him evicted, he would set out to get himself arrested by the police and housed at their expense. Spring, summer and autumn his preferred place of residence was the doorway of a large Boots' store in the city centre. When sober he would sweep up the front of the store as a sort of rental charge. At those times he would chat amicably even though he gave little away about himself.

On those occasions when his funds did not stretch to drinking himself into a comatose state his temper was short and likely to be explosive. There were regular complaints about his offensive and abusive words and behaviour sometimes accompanied by allegations of assaults on passing members of the public by means of his walking stick.

Unlike most street living 'plonkeys' Rowan had a 'girlfriend' and in summer they were almost inseparable. Loaded down with full carrier bags they still managed to hold hands as they made their way to and from the town centre park.

On one occasion (at least) with blossom on the trees, daisies and buttercups on the lawns and the fountains playing under a blue-sky Rowan became aroused. His partner, Doris, must have welcomed the attentions of her aroused beau and they soon became involved in sexual activity. Sadly, for the loving pair the place they chose for the happy event was immediately in front of the Police Headquarters. It took place in full view of all those enjoying lunch in the canteen of that building. The audience grew and there were cheers and woops until at last someone decided that enough was enough. Rowan and Doris were dragged apart and taken into custody.

I had not witnessed the event as I was working in the custody office that day and booked both the disgruntled offenders in. I could not imagine how they had indulged in sex through the layers of clothes they both wore but I was assured by them that that indeed was what they had been doing.

Somewhere along the way Doris disappeared from Rowans' life and if alcohol and street living were not enough, his downward spiral accelerated.

I remember vividly one meeting I had with him when I was very young in service. I was working an 'early turn' (0600hours to 1400hours) and I was 'doubled up' (working with another officer). We were standing near to a busy road junction where we would be seen by lots of members of the public, even if we were not doing an awful lot.

Traffic was flowing slowly but steadily as people headed towards their places of work. We had not witnessed anything which required our attention until, suddenly, a lane of traffic stuttered to a halt. In 'plod speak' car horns are known a "audible warning instruments" and all at once lots of them were being blown. The cause of this was a drunken and aggressive Rowan making his way across the busy road.

He waved his walking stick, shouted abuse, dropped his carrier bags and picked them up again as he meandered his way across four lanes of traffic. There is no doubt that Rowan constituted a nuisance to other road users but the speed of the traffic and the nature of his progress represented little danger to anyone.

We waited for him as he staggered his way towards us. He was obviously in a bad mood caused, no doubt, by a bad nights' sleep and the absence of his first cider of the day. Suddenly a voice boomed from behind us.

"Officers! Arrest that man."

We both turned and there was one of the rarest sights to be seen in those days. A police superintendent, in full uniform, out of his office at eight o' clock in the morning and bearing down on us like a ship under full sail.

"It's Rowan Martin, Sir." Stuttered my companion. "We try not to arrest him. He's….."

The superintendent would hear no more.

"Arrest that man and arrest him now!"

So, we did and Rowan was as stunned as we were, he lapsed into total silence. It was probably the earliest in the morning he had ever been arrested and definitely the only time he had been arrested when totally sober. We chatted with him amicably as we waited for a van to convey him to the police station. The superintendent stood there shuffling from foot to foot, clearly unsettled at being in contact with the public and constables at this time in the morning.

Our arrival at the station was not greeted with anything approaching enthusiasm. The staff were busy getting those prisoners who had been held overnight ready to attend court and we had to sit and wait and wait and wait. At last, the sergeant called us to his counter.

"Who is the arresting officer?" Asked the sergeant.

Before we could say anything, Rowan interjected,

"He's not here, is he?"

The sergeant waited for an explanation but Rowan was on a roll.

"He was the posh nob with the gold on his cap. He should be here."

This was both amusing and embarrassing as the sergeant now demanded that the superintendent should be brought to the Custody Office. Superintendents were even less to be spotted in Custody Offices than they were to be seen on streets. We would be held responsible for his being brought to this 'dirty place'.

On his entering the sergeants' domain his distaste at being there was immediately evident. He sniffed the air which reeked of body odour, blocked drains and unwashed socks. He walked backwards and forwards in much the same way as caged prisoners do in the exercise area and he deliberately avoided making eye contact with Rowan or us.

It was decided, after much discussion between the superintendent and the sergeant that there was no power of arrest for 'jay walking'. As usual the fall-back charge of being drunk and disorderly was chosen. This, however, did not go down well with Rowan.

"I am not drunk." He exploded. "I am an expert on drunk. I have not had a drink this morning. You can't prove it this time. Take me to court now and let the judges decide."

There was a further quiet chat between the two persons of supervising rank. The sergeant then addressed Rowan,

"You have been arrested for Breach of the Peace. You will be kept here until the roads are quieter and safer for you and them then let out. Would you like breakfast.?"

Rowan would definitely like breakfast and things appeared to heading towards a happy resolution when the superintendent interposed.

"Officers. Search this man and place him in a cell."

Rowan was filthy, after decades of street sleeping, and the superintendent was probably just exerting his authority as a means of getting his own back. We searched the pockets of Rowans' overcoat and found string, coins, a toilet roll, some pebbles, a can opener and assorted sweet papers. He removed his overcoat to reveal another coat which was even grubbier than the first one. We searched the second garment and found almost identical items there as in the first one. The pile of items steadily rose on the custody office desk.

Under the second coat was a sports jacket, two woollen jumpers and a shirt that had once been white. Each layer was removed so that the next could be properly searched under the hawk eye of the superintendent. Step by step Rowan seemed to diminish like the Russian Dolls.

Finally, Rowan stood there in what I believe are called "woolly coms.", a sort of all-in-one vest and under pant item with sleeves and legs. I cannot imagine when this item had last seen the light of day. The groin area of the garment was stained a yellowish colour while the rest of it was a greyish brown and grey which with numerous stains gave it a tie and dye appearance.

As he stood there in his large black boots and soiled underwear, I felt a pang of sympathy for what was essentially a frail old man. I also, guiltily, wondered again how he and Doris had engaged in so much sexual activity if he was encased in so many layers of clothes.

"There are pockets in that thing." Gloated the superintendent, as he pointed at Rowans' undergarment.

I put my hand in the pocket and felt something warm and damp. As I removed the item from its' hiding place, I held what looked like a decayed, amputated finger. It had a brown, uneven surface with flecks of green on it and an overall damp sheen as if it were sweating.

The superintendent moved over to get a closer look as I started to notice a vague smell of decay. Suddenly Rowan grabbed the item from me.

"That's my sausage," he stated, as he plunged the thing into his mouth. The very thought of how long the item had been there festering in his underpants made me feel queasy. The superintendent slumped onto the bench which ran along the custody office wall. He looked ashen and certainly wished he had not initiated the thorough search.

Some years passed before I saw Rowan again. By that time, I had moved to a different police area. I patrolled a beat that included several streets of terraced, red brick houses that had been lined up for demolition. They had their doors and windows boarded up for safety and security reasons but as time passed many of the boards had been removed and stolen.

The terraced houses had once formed part of a thriving community but now it resembled a ghost town. Every now and then a convoy of travellers' vehicles would arrive and often secure free electric by wiring their caravans up to the street lights. Their presence was the reason for my being there one cold November night.

The travellers did not appear to be in residence when I visited but an orangey glow flickered from one of the derelict houses. I clambered over a pile of rubbish in the doorway of the illuminated building. As I entered, I could smell smoke and heard the crackling of burning wood. There was also a strange smell that did not fit with a domestic fire.

In what had been the living room of the house a wooden railway sleeper had been placed with its end in the open fireplace. That end of the tar-soaked piece of wood was blazing merrily.

Sat on a chair with his legs resting on the sleeper was a comatose male person. It could have been a cosy scene but for the fact that flames had spread along the sleeper and ignited the man's trousers and boots. I quickly recognized the man as Rowan. There were several empty cider bottles spread around his sleeping place and no amount of shouting was going to rouse him.

Grabbing Rowans' shoulders, I dragged him out of the building and into the cold night air. He was still unconscious when I put his burning boots and trousers out with the blanket from my patrol car. Further he was still out for the count when an ambulance arrived and conveyed him to the nearest hospital.

Rowan could have burned to death that night, but strangely the incident undoubtedly saved him. His burns were serious but treatable, however, the other leg had areas of gangrenous flesh that, left to themselves, could well have killed him. The nurse who was on ward duty when I visited Rowan told me that fleas had burrowed into his skin, he had scratched and the wounds had become badly infected.

I know that Rowan survived the burns and the removal of the gangrenous tissue but I never saw him again. In a strange way I missed him. I regularly claim that society is made up of good, bad and dodgy people but for me Rowan was none of those things, he was a victim of society, a wasted life but a real character.

CHAPTER NINE

VICE

On the fourth of July 1975 a woman of Irish extraction, who had married a Polish man, decided to go to a nightclub in Bradford. Anna Rogulsky was a resident of Keighley, my home town, and she lived not far from what had been my first school in the town. Having separated from her husband she now lived with a boyfriend but he had no desire to go night clubbing on the occasion in question, he decided not to accompany her to the bright lights of the big city and remained in Keighley. By midnight Anna was also feeling that it was time for home and secured a lift with two Jamaican men. She got home safe and sound but her boyfriend was not at her house as she had expected. Irritated by this she decided that she would go and visit him at his alternative residence which was about quarter of a mile away.

She walked downhill into the centre of Keighley, crossed North Street, one of the two main roads dissecting the town and proceeded towards the Ritz Cinema on Alice Street. (In earlier years I had visited the Ritz every Saturday morning to watch Flash Gordon or the Lone Ranger defeat their respective enemies.) She then passed down a narrow alley at the back of the picture house before arriving at the row of terraced houses where her boyfriend lived.

As she tried to rouse him by banging on his door and windows, neighbours heard the commotion and lay wondering what to do. Anna was about to return home when she received a sudden and violent blow to the back of her head. There were at least two more blows either from the Cuban heel of the attacker's shoe or some other blunt and heavy object. The attacker may have gone on to commit further violent actions against his fallen victim but he was disturbed by one of the neighbours who had, at last, decided to ascertain the cause of all the noise

Anna's body was discovered some time later. She was still alive and quickly came to be regarded as a victim of Peter Sutcliffe, the 'Yorkshire Ripper.' She was not the first woman that Sutcliffe attacked and she was far from being the last. She was not even the only person to be attacked by him in or near Keighley. It has been suggested that Sutcliffe killed far more people than the thirteen whose murders he was convicted for. It has also been suggested that he operated over a much wider area than was thought at the time and that at least two of his victims may have been men. What is certain is that by the late 1970's people in the Leeds/Bradford area of Yorkshire were living in an apprehensive and fearful state.

I do not mention the Yorkshire Ripper here because I played any part in his apprehension. I did work for a man who had a major role in questioning him and my father was interviewed because his car had the same type of tyres as those that had left tracks at one of the murder scenes. However, Sutcliffe appears here because he directly affected my working life over a number of months.

One of the roles of the Plainclothes Unit to which I found myself attached was to monitor and where necessary bring cases against prostitutes. This usually involved sitting in an unmarked police car and watching the 'girls' approach passing motorists or offenders. If they approached two or more men then we could take them in and caution them and once cautioned if they did the same again, we could put them before the magistrates where they would be declared 'common prostitutes' and fined. Most of the women did not greatly resent us 'policing' them, provided it was done fairly and they were put before the court 'in turn'.

With the 'Ripper' on the prowl the 'girls' became even friendlier towards us. We were a form of insurance in that we knew when they were picked up and we monitored the vehicle registration numbers of cars that were 'cruising' the area. The number of prostitutes put before the court declined at this time. Some of them may have stopped working the streets but the real reason was that we started to focus on the men who frequented the area in the hope of catching the 'big cheese' himself.

As far as I know, Peter Sutcliffe never visited the red-light area in which I was working. There was, however, something of a stir when one of the senior officers from my Force was found driving round a West Yorkshire area frequented by prostitutes. He must have behaved suspiciously because the officers who stopped him searched his car and underneath the driver's seat, they found a mask. Not just any mask, this was a black leather affair like a hood with a zip where the mouth would be and slit holes for the eyes. I believe this sort of mask is regularly used in those venues which specialize in 'bondage'. In any event it was not the sort of gear to be cruising a red-light area with at the time of the Yorkshire Ripper.

The officer told those who questioned him that he was conducting research for a book he was planning. I do not know what role the mask was to have had in the book but I do know that his career never really recovered and wherever he went there were sniggers and asides such as "Who is that masked man?" or "They're all the same with a mask on!".

It was not permitted to "watch" the girls on your own so we worked in pairs and my usual partner was an officer called Monty. This was not his real name. Monty spoke with the accent of a member of the landed gentry, indeed most of his traits and habits did not belong in the environment of a police station. He wore tweed jackets, doeskin waistcoats and flannel trousers with heavy brogue shoes completing the picture. He did not drink beer, which was unheard of in the Police Service of that era; indeed, there was a legend that at a social event the bar order had been twelve pints of beer for the men and a sweet sherry for Monty.

The strange thing was that he was not a member of the landed classes at all. Before joining the Police, he had worked as a salesman selling tractors and other agricultural equipment and he left that because his wife could not manage on the money.

Monty was immensely 'hen pecked', if you are allowed to use that expression nowadays. In the office one day I heard his wife haranguing him on the telephone. His 'crime' was to have eaten a KitKat biscuit and only left one in the tin. In consequence when the wife's friend had come round for tea she could not be properly provided for. Poor old Monty even offered to drive home with another biscuit but forgiveness was not forthcoming and he spent the shift apprehensively chewing his finger nails and wondering what she would do when he got home.

I tried not to go in pubs with Monty. I found it embarrassing, he was a ship out of water and he drew attention to us even when the aim was to blend in. There was a pub, called the Eagle and Child on our red-light patch. Now it is a listed building and people flock to enjoy its olde worlde charms and fine ales from around the world. Then, quite frankly, it was a dump with character. The prostitutes gathered there before and during work so 'punters' and 'pimps' also arrived in number. The landlord added to the ambience by having a semi-nude dancing girl gyrating in a cage near the toilets and walking around with a parrot on his shoulder. I was told that he used to have two parrots but a customer, now barred, had bitten the head off the second bird.

One night, as we sat in a Ford Fiesta watching the girls, a large black man walked past us. He was about six feet four inches tall and nearly as broad. His face was pock marked and scarred. This was Max Ramsden a one-man crime wave who, when not thieving or serving time, lived off the earnings of his female partner and her sister. Those earnings came from plying their trade as street prostitutes.

Immediately Monty was on the radio asking if Ramsden was currently wanted. It transpired that he was and I immediately started to feel as if the air had been let out of my balloon. Nothing good was going to come from approaching Max Ramsden and doing that with Monty rendered the whole exercise hazardous. I refused to go into the pub, which was my colleagues preferred option, as there was not a single person in there with any love for the Police. We decided to wait for him to come out and I added that we should then immediately ask for back up from uniform officers.

About an hour later Ramsden lurched out of the pub like a slowly moving mountain. Down went the window at Monty's side of the car, "I want you Ramsden", he shouted. Before either of us could get out or radio for help our target came to the car and placed his hands on the roof. It was as if he were challenging us to do something but then his patience failed him. He rocked the car gently a couple of times and with a massive effort he flipped it onto its side. I could not believe what I had experienced. Monty who had been in the passenger seat was now sprawled on top of me and showing no signs of getting off. I could smell petrol and I could see a crowd of people emerging from the pub. Fortunately, no one threw a cigarette or a match and we managed to clamber out. Ramsden had lost interest and had gone off to beat his girlfriend up. More officers arrived and we righted the car which proved drivable. The rest of the shift was spent doing paperwork to explain what had happened and with me failing a sense of humour test when a sergeant told me I was suspended from driving because I had been involved in a police vehicle accident!

Max Ramsden was not what you would call a 'star criminal'. He was not a thinker who planned sophisticated heists, he was a blunt weapon who relied on opportunity and physical force. In his later years as his strength dwindled, he became a slightly pathetic figure. On one occasion he was found hiding in a wardrobe, not because he thought the Police were coming but because he feared someone, he had threatened was actually too big for him.

Les Saltonstall was a slightly different sort of criminal. He was not particularly tall but he was extremely broad and muscular. His blond hair sat on top of a high, almost Neanderthal, forehead and he had hands like small shovels. Not possessed of the greatest of intellects, Les relied on his brothers to do the thinking for him and it was as a whole family that the star criminal categorization could be applied to the Saltonstall's. Les, Billy, Brian and Craig were a formidable quartet who had tried almost every sort of crime but had decided to specialise in armed robbery.

By the time I joined the Police Force the 'glory days' of the Saltonstall's were long over. However, they still found themselves as the 'usual suspects' every time there was a robbery within fifty miles of their homes. One evening towards the end of 1978 information was received that a Greek restaurant was to be burgled and a safe on the premises was to be stolen or blown. The information was supposed to be reliable and as usual the Saltonstall's were thought to be the most likely offenders.

It was with that background that I found myself on a cold November evening on the top floor of a Georgian house that functioned as a Solicitor's office. From the window of the room, that I occupied with a colleague, we could look down onto the roof and frontage of the Greek restaurant. We had night vision glasses that enabled us to see through the gloom, a thermos flask filled with tepid tomato soup and a bag of chicken sandwiches.

Over the years I took part in a number of observations and I cannot recall one instance where I witnessed anything vaguely resembling the activity that was expected to take place. This evening was no exception. The minutes ticked by slowly and gradually formed themselves into hours. Nothing was happening. There were not even any casual passers-by. Then, a little after midnight a car pulled onto the piece of spare land at the side of the restaurant. My heart raced, we reported the action to our radio controllers and watched as quietly as possible.

Two figures emerged from the car and walked into the roadway between the restaurant and the building in which we were hidden. One of the figures was undoubtedly female and her high heeled shoes clicked loudly enough on the cobbled road for us to hear from our place of concealment. Together they made their way not towards the restaurant but to the Solicitor's office from which we were watching them.

We heard the door open down below and the click clicking of the shoes in the hallway. Then we heard muffled voices and the sound of steps being taken on the wooden, uncarpeted staircase. After a moments panic, fearing that the two people would climb right to our position, all went quiet. Then, after a few minutes, we heard a rhythmic bumping from the office underneath our position. Looking back, I should have known what was happening but at the time my colleague and I were thinking 'crime' and our conclusion was that some sort of theft was taking place literally underneath our noses.

I crept down the flight of stairs from our position to the floor beneath. A shaft of light shone weakly through a partially open office door. I crawled along the foot of the office wall towards the light, hardly daring to breath but noticing that the bumping was getting louder. On my hands and knees, I peered round the frame of the door and into the office. I immediately wished I was somewhere else.!

A partially clad female lay on her back across the desk situated in the middle of the office. Her legs were at either side of a standing male figure who was thrusting in and out of her as if his life depended on it. The women belonged in the office, or at least I knew her to be a member of the firm who occupied the premises. The man was Les Saltonstall wearing only a vest and with his trousers round his ankles.

I found it difficult to stop looking but I was also fearful of being seen. We had found Les within the width of a road from where we had expected to find him but he certainly had an alibi on this occasion. I crawled back to my colleague and told him what I had seen, we then had to wait until the figures finished their 'business' and left. We were sworn to secrecy as this was the sort of story that would have spread like wildfire in a police station and no doubt in the criminal underground if it had reached that far.

I was to meet Les Saltonstall again over a year later. After two years at my first police station, I had asked for a move and transferred to a smaller, more rural base. One day a 'friend' who was a fellow member of the Force Athletics team asked me if I would drop off a bunch of flowers at his girlfriend's house. The house was in the area I worked in whereas he was based two or three miles away. It seemed a fairly normal friendly thing to do. At least it felt like that until the door of the house I was delivering to opened. There, once again wearing a vest and with his muscles rippling, was Les. I stood there on the doorstep in full uniform holding a bunch of red roses. I blurted out that the flowers were a community prize and he looked at me as if his brain might take some time to consider that information. I left immediately and as I looked back; he was still standing on the doorstep holding the roses.

What goes around comes around, or so they say, Les had been having an affair with the solicitor and his wife was doing the same with the detective constable who had almost dropped me in it. I have waited a long time to get my own back but the opportunity has not arisen.... yet!

I went back into uniform shortly after the live sex show and soon experienced an event that made me wonder what made senior officers tick. I had worked all Christmas but was due to be off on New Year's Eve. I had paid a substantial amount of money to attend an all you could eat and drink event at a rugby club and I was supposed to be stopping at a friend's house.

My shift on New Year's Eve started at 0700hours and was due to finish eight hours later at 1500 hours. Just after noon it started to snow. Big fluffy flakes that drifted down and settled on you and everything round and about. It quickly became the sort of weather that everyone loves to see at Christmas and which has a cheery beauty if you are watching it from inside with a log fire blazing away in the hearth. In a city centre with wet feet and frozen fingers it has a wholly different aspect.

Just before I started heading back to the station to go off duty, I heard an alarm sounding at the Debenhams Store. The shop had closed early because of the weather, though I suspected a departing member of staff may have triggered the alarm. On my arrival the premises were in darkness, the main doors locked. However, there was a gaping hole in the first window I came to, this was either a break in or a deliberate damage. I called Control and asked for a key holder to be called out and some back up to help secure the building.

A Dog Handler arrived soon after me but he would not put his dog into the shop as there was broken glass on the floor inside. So, we waited and we waited and we waited. It went dark and felt to have got colder but the snow continued, the number of vehicles driving passed the shop seemed to be dwindling and the depth of snow and slush was gradually increasing.

No keyholder arrived but eventually a red faced and rotund toby jug of an inspector waddled up to myself and the dog handler.

"Are all sides of the building covered? He asked.

"No, Sir," I replied and continued, "this happened at shift turnover time and control had no more staff to send."

"So why are you both stood here holding hands?"

"All other doors and windows are secure and we cannot cover all four sides."

"Right. I'll go and have some tea then."

I could not believe he had said it. I was on duty four hours after I should have gone home. My feet were soaked, my fingers numb and he was going for a cup of tea!

"How long will I be required.?" I asked, trying not to sound on the edge of rebellion.

"Till you're stood down." He answered abruptly.

I told him that I was supposed to be going to a social function and that I had already been on duty for twelve hours and he seemed momentarily put off his stride. Then his face darkened and I thought he was going to explode.

"There is a reason why you are a PC," he shouted, "and you will always be a PC if you carry on like this."

He started to walk away and then he turned back to us.

"In five years, I will be a Chief Officer and you could still be standing here for all I fucking care.!"

He then strode off, his breath like the steam from a kettle in the cold night air. After about ten yards he paused to check the traffic before crossing the road and as he did so he slipped and fell in the slush. I could have cheered and neither my colleague nor I rushed to his aid. He tried to get up, slipped again and seemed to be flapping around like a penguin as the snowflakes fell on him.

An hour later I was relieved by another PC who told me that I could go off duty. All trains out of the city had stopped and I was lucky to catch the last bus. As the warmth of my transport's heater reached my toes and fingers steam rose off me in wet clouds. I was lost in thoughts of what I would like to do to the inspector but it was to be several years before I got any sense of satisfaction in that direction.

The inspector went on to achieve the rank of Assistant Chief Constable and transferred from my Force to another some hundred miles or so to the south. He was appointed to the post of ACC(Operations) and amongst his duties was a responsibility to oversee the Traffic Department. Keen to make an early impact on his arrival he decided to visit the Motorway Traffic Unit. He sat in his nice warm office for an hour or so and then discovered the internal phone directory. He rang the Force's Control Room and asked for a car to take him to the Motorway Unit. Ten minutes later there was no car waiting for him so he rang again and was put through to a sergeant.

The conversation must have seemed strange to both parties. My former antagonist asked for a car and the sergeant asked if, he was sure. This must have seemed extremely annoying to the former inspector who would be full of his own importance and so he again demanded a car. The sergeant again asked if he was sure and an explosive temper tantrum cannot have been far away.

At last, the sergeant caved in and said a car would be sent immediately and sure enough a few minutes later a large three litre engined Traffic Car pulled up outside the building that housed the ACC's office. In full uniform he marched out to meet his driver who merely opened the back door to let his passenger get in. The car moved off steadily took the first left turn, then three more left turns before pulling up exactly where it had started from.

The driver then informed the ACC that the Motorway Unit was on the second floor almost directly above his own office. I was not there so I do not know if the former inspector kept calm or not. I did, however, experience a warm glow when I heard the story some months later. Yet, although this incident confirmed my view of the man, his character had not prevented his having climbed up the Police hierarchy.

A few years later, when I was on a course at the Police Staff College in Hampshire (of which more later), I found out that he had resigned from the Service following a security breach. He had apparently been involved in the planning of a high security event and had taken the papers home with him. That was not strictly permissible but leaving them in a taxi was almost unforgivable. The papers were handed to a newspaper and I suppose the rest is history. Strangely I had a better feeling when he appeared as a buffoon in search of the Motorway Unit than I did when he was just human; revenge was not totally satisfying.

I also had a more serious run in with another senior officer during my probation. When I was first allowed to patrol by myself, I was given a regular beat and became very attached to it. I came to know every nook and crevice, every tea spot and all the people who might have useful information. One such 'informant' was a little Irishman who sold evening newspapers from the steps of a former bank. He would tie one copy of the paper to the pillar at the side of the huge door of the old building. I would stand on the steps with him and he would tell me where shoplifters went with their stolen goods and where small drug deals were taking place. Perhaps more importantly in the days before texts and the internet he used to tell me the latest score in cricket matches involving Yorkshire County Cricket Club.

One day I was a little late, he was tidying up and, in a hurry, to be on his way. He told me he had not had chance to look at the score but the paper he had tied to the pillar was a latest edition. He said it was destined for the bin as it was torn and I could put it there for him after checking how my team were doing. I thanked him, folded the tatty paper and put it in my tunic pocket. Moments later I was called to the station to take a statement from someone who had been involved in a traffic collision.

As I sat in one of the station's interview rooms trying to get a feel for the events that the witness wanted to tell me about, a superintendent opened the door and asked to speak to me. Once in the corridor and away from the interview room he asked me for the stolen goods that I had in my possession. I was staggered and, genuinely, I had no idea what he was talking about. Only after he mentioned the newspaper did I take it from my tunic pocket and I was never to see it again. He told me the paper did not belong to the Irishman and, therefore, I was either stealing or handling stolen goods. He said my career was over.

Now to put this episode in context I must point out that in the 1970's superintendents were hardly ever seen by constables.

They were the occupants of some sort of 'other world' which mere mortals avoided. Thus, if a superintendent said something to me it must be true and I really believed I was about to be sacked. He sent me home and told me not to come back to work until I heard from him. I did what most of my colleagues would have done, I went to the pub.

The majority of people who join the police remain constables for the entirety of their careers and some of them become experts on surviving by doing as little as possible. These individuals are usually termed "barrack room" lawyers. They have seen it all before and are quick to tell you what you should do. In the pub I quickly had a small audience of them who bombarded me with advice. The most helpful pointed out that if the newspaper seller actually had a right to the papers there could be no offence. So, we went en masse to try and find my little Irish chum. This attempt to take positive action backfired because as we arrived, he was getting into what was very clearly a police car driven by a plainclothes officer.

I spent two days worrying and fretting about what was going to happen and finally received a phone call asking me to call at the Assistant Chief Constable's Office. This, I thought, was it. I was about to be sacked. I stood in the corridor outside the ACC's office for nearly half an hour and when I when I got to see him, he told me that the dates for my Special Course had come through. He could not understand why I did not seem excited and I did not explain why I was in a state of total shock.

As I left the Chief Officer's corridor the superintendent who had taken the paper was waiting on the stairs. He told me I could come back to work and that it transpired the Irishman bought the papers he sold and that, therefore, I had not committed an offence. He stressed though that police officers should not receive gifts and that he would be watching me in the future.

At the time I was just relieved that the whole incident was over. I felt in one way that I had learned a lesson, certainly you never knew who was watching you when you walked the streets in a uniform. As the years went by and I became aware of what some people got away with I resented having been made to feel so humiliated over a newspaper. The superintendent went on to discipline an officer for not wearing his helmet when he was rescuing a child from a pond but he came unstuck himself some years later.

In the quest for promotion, he transferred to a southern Force and bought a large house in the countryside. One day he was visited by a van load of travellers who offered to tarmac his drive for half the price he had been quoted by a legitimate company. The work was done, but in places the tarmac was so thin that you could almost see through it. After a fall out over payment the superintendent was hit over the head with a shovel. When he regained consciousness, it became clear that he had suffered some serious damage. He did return to work but after a short time had to retire on the grounds of ill health. I got no satisfaction from what could only be described as a tragedy.

I could write chapter after chapter about disciplinary matters and I am afraid that there will be more about them if you read on. However, I think there has been enough gloomy stuff for a while and maybe it's time to go to the pub!

CHAPTER TEN

BEER

I have spent a considerable portion of my adult life in and around pubs. I have drunk copious quantities of beer in them, worked serving beer in them and latterly been responsible for enforcing the law relating to them. It is one area where I could claim to be a 'poacher turned gamekeeper'. However, it is my experience that if you like drinking beer you can never really be on the side of the angels in relation to licensed premises!

I will start here by telling you about a landlord who blamed me for all his troubles. His pub was a large building in a small market town, it had a huge car park and beer garden and had once been a coaching inn and hotel. The town had four pubs, a restaurant and two working men's clubs. What customers there were had a lot of choice and they spread themselves thinly.

The landlords of the various premises tried everything they could to attract business. They sold Bar Meals cheaper than you could cook at home, they held Quiz Nights, Karaoke, Folk Concerts, Race Nights and every sort of legitimate event that pubs could host. Yet, in spite of the imaginative offerings the various premises struggled to make money in substantial quantities. One or two of them fell back on that old, tried and tested, method of supplementing takings, that is, they served after the end of legal drinking hours.

These 'lock ins' were undoubtedly what kept the offending landlords in business. A few heavy drinkers, sat round an ill lit bar for a couple of hours, can consume a good quantity of ale and supplement a night's takings no end. My problem was that I lived directly opposite the main offender in the town and while I could turn a blind eye to some of the after-hours drinking, I could not ignore the noise and street disturbances. I had the pub visited regularly and the landlord was on a last warning.

The fact that the landlord was taking matters at a personal level became apparent in a strange way. The town had an annual Scarecrow Competition. Local residents would make a scarecrow and create a scene where their creations would assume a sense of reality. For example, in the churchyard a bride and groom could be seen being photographed; they and the 'photographer' were scarecrows. Next to the village pond a fisherman sat watching his float and enjoying a tin of beer, there was no sign of the straw that padded out his clothes or face mask. Everywhere you looked a scarecrow was doing something and some of them were absolutely wonderful.

From the chimney pot of the pub opposite my house, with its neck locked in the embrace of a noose, dangled the scarecrow image of a police superintendent. It was quite a good representation, the cap had gold braid on it, the uniform tunic had a crown and the shoes were quite shiny. I found out later some of the uniform had been borrowed from a fireman. For several weeks, every time I left my house there was my effigy hanging from the chimney. In November it was no longer there, the scarecrow served as the 'Guy' at the pub's bonfire.

I never succeeded in closing the pub. The landlord did that himself. One night after an evening drinking with his cronies he decided that it was his wife's turn to be put in her place. Shouts and screams could be heard throughout the village and in the early hours the landlord was taken away in handcuffs while the wife was conveyed to hospital for treatment to headwounds. In the pub residential accommodation, a scenes of crime officer recovered part of the scalp of the wife from the side of the bath.

The landlord went to prison, the wife applied for and obtained a liquor licence for her to run the pub and I moved out of the town. In a strange way I miss the scarecrows!

Several years earlier I had found late opening pubs much more humorous and enjoyable. There was a short period of time when I decided to live close to the sea even though it was miles from my place of work. One evening while trying out a new car I came across a pub on a remote stretch of coastline. It was like something from a different age. The advertisements behind the bar were for brands of beer that had long disappeared and the records on the juke box were from two decades prior to my arrival.

The landlord was a tall thin man with mutton chop sideburns and thinning mousey hair. The few locals, who mainly sat on stools at the bar, referred to him as "the Gaffer" and I never heard him called anything else. On my second visit I ordered a bar meal and the steak and chips that arrived would have been worthy of an Egon Ronay restaurant. I became a regular and on occasion I called in on my way home from work, when licensed premises should have been closed.

One afternoon I arrived at the pub, it was well after the time that the pub should have been closed. To my amazement the doors to the front and rear of the premises were closed and apparently locked. I was sure that I could see the Gaffer wandering around inside though he showed no sign of hearing me knock on the doors.

I was about to leave when a local made his way to the front door.

"He won't open up, you know? He's been scared off. Thirty years I've been coming here and he's never shut on time once. Yesterday he did it for the first time and it took a dozen coppers with machine guns to make him do it!"

I found out later that the Police Firearms Team had been training on the beach and were making their way back to their vans further down the road. One of the officers decided to see if the pub had any sandwiches and the Gaffer saw armed men assembling on his car park. Apparently, according to his own admission, he hid under a table until they all left. No amount of rational argument could persuade him that the officers had not turned up specifically to prevent his offending.

My next experience with drinking after hours could have got me in serious trouble. That it didn't was down to a pragmatic constable who probably did not want to end up with a pile of paperwork. At the time I was living in a small village with three working farms along the road it was built around. There were two pubs, one of which did excellent food and was prone to a little "afters".

One evening I was supposed to attend a party in the city which was being held to celebrate the promotion of one of my staff. To avoid the temptation of drinking and driving my wife drove me to the venue for the social event. She then went to visit a friend and told me to ring her there when I was ready for home. The friend's telephone number was written down on a piece of paper and everything should have been straightforward. After an hour or so I got a little bored and I can remember rubbing the paper, with the phone number on it, between my fingers. Eventually I decided I had had enough and went to a phone box (pre mobile days) and it was only then I realized I had rubbed the number out.

I decided that the best thing to do was to get a taxi home and wait for my wife there. When I arrived back in our village, I realized that I did not have a key for the house. I could have gone to the pub immediately but decided to try and get in the house and leave a message for my wife. I got the ladders that we kept at the bottom of the garden and took them to the front of the house, knowing that the bedroom window upstairs was open. I climbed in, left a note, got some more money and made my way to the pub arriving about ten minutes before closing time. Two or three pints later and well after closing time the pub was in full swing when there was a knock on the front door. When the landlord opened it there were two police officers on the door step.

To my embarrassment they asked for me by name! Outside the pub I was told that a neighbour had reported seeing a man climb into my house. The officers had arrived and found the ladders still up to an open window. One of them had entered my house and, finding no one in, he had shut the window and put the ladder in the gardens. I explained what had happened, though I could not remember leaving the ladders on the footpath, anyone could have climbed in. No one ever mentioned this incident to me but I am sure stories about the drunken superintendent would have been circulating the junior ranks for some time.

It may be fair to say that I have been guilty of inappropriate behaviour in pubs more often than I have been the victim of landlord's actions towards me. However, for the most part I have been an interested observer of the activities of others and in my early days as a police officer there was plenty to watch.

At least once a month there would be a 'relief do', a get together where anything could happen. We usually hired a private room at a pub or club and it is probably as well that we did. On one occasion an officer set fire to the curtains in a city centre pub because his girlfriend had jilted him; on another occasion a high-ranking Mormon Church official turned up to excommunicate an inebriated female church member whose behaviour was considered to be unacceptable. However, some of the most memorable happenings were often not wrong in any way.

Bert Dickinson was a sergeant in the control room of the station I worked at. He was a tall slim man with hair of a silvery grey colour. He seemed too old to be a police officer and he moved stiffly and robotically. He seldom smiled and gave the impression of thinking deeply before he made any decision. Having said all that, he was a pleasant enough man who attended relief functions regularly but usually sat quietly in a corner and only spoke if he was spoken to. Wherever the monthly event was held Bert would wear the same grey suit, blue tie and polished shoes with his hair brushed back from his forehead in a Teddy Boy like quiff.

Bert did, however, have a liking for young policewomen. He did not pursue them but he was very protective of them in a chivalrous, old-world sort of way. One young officer, Diane Griffiths, was even newer in the job than I was, she was so small you could easily miss her but she had beautiful eyes and they clearly captivated Bert. Every chance he got Bert would have Diane working in the control room to keep her safe and he would offer to share his sandwiches with her in a way that was not unnoticed by the other staff.

Diane was not happy. She was homesick and desperately wanted to transfer to the South Wales Force. She had been a keen dancer before joining the Police and grumbled that she had met no one who could move properly since she had left the valleys of Wales. The sadder Diane became the more protective and fatherlier Bert became but he never stepped beyond the boundaries of acceptability.

One month the get together was held in the function room of a large city centre pub. A DJ had been hired and everyone had chipped in for a buffet. A large number of officers turned up, many with their partners and some from other reliefs. Copious amounts of alcohol were consumed and the music seemed to get louder and louder. I noticed Bert sat by himself and also noticed that he was wearing a raincoat but that did not register with me as unusual. I suppose I just thought he was not intending to stop long or did not want to risk leaving his coat in the cloakroom.

After a couple of hours, a number of people started to dance and I remember hearing the opening strains of Saturday Night Fever being played. This was still all the rage at the time and more people made their way onto the dance floor. I saw Bert walking to the table that Diane was sat at and a brief conversation took place between him and her. She stood up and Bert, still in his coat, led her towards the dancers. Just before he started dancing, he took off the raincoat and draped it across a chair.

He was wearing a one-piece outfit made of some shiny green material that glittered under the bright lights in the dance room. The top of his outfit was open from his neck to his waist and a mat of greying chest hair was amply displayed. One by one the dancers came to a halt shocked by the appearance of their control room sergeant. Even Diane looked like she did not know whether to laugh or cry but eventually she started to move to the music. Bert had clearly learned the steps and he strutted and swayed across the floor like a demented android. At the appropriate moment his arm shot into the air in mimicry of John Travolta's salute and at the same time the crutch of his outfit split.

Bert dashed to the side of the dancefloor and put his raincoat on. He then escorted Diane back to her table and went back to his own lonely seat. Everyone was in total shock. Had we witnessed the courting ritual of a dirty old man or the genuine attempt by a gentleman to make a lonely girl happier?

It transpired that Bert had been taking dancing lessons for weeks in the build-up to his 'performance'. It was a one night only special that was never repeated. Diane went back to Wales and Bert got on with being a control room sergeant but in my opinion, he had a made a tremendous gesture.

Almost all the police officers that I met in my early days liked to have a drink. Most of them would, however, admit that the CID get togethers were the most memorable. One Christmas Eve event held in Police Headquarters became so rowdy that the Chief Constable turned up in person and closed the bar!

As the Chief Constable was playing at being a real police officer two detectives, within twenty meters of him, were definitely not behaving like police officers. One of the two entrances/exits to the bar and recreation room at Headquarters was reached at the top of a flight of stairs, the other led onto a short corridor at the end of which was a shower room with a six-shower unit behind a long nylon curtain. The two male detectives were indulging in the worst sort of behaviour usually associated with office Christmas parties.

One of the officers, Tony Ikstrum, was a close friend of mine. His parents were of Ukranian abstraction though he had been born in our Force area. He had only recently joined the CID and from the moment he had done so he had been pursued by the daughter of one of the station Detective Inspectors. She worked in an office in the Headquarters Building but was now with Tony indulging in naughty behaviour in the showers.

After the midday sexual shenanigans were terminated, but before Tony had chance to book off duty, he heard a voice calling his name. The voice was clearly that of the Detective Inspector whose daughter Tony had recently been getting to know.

"Iksrum, my office. Now!" The voice boomed and reverberated down the corridor and plunged Tony into a state of total panic. Should he try to sneak out? How could he explain what he had just done? Had the girl admitted the events to her father and claimed it all to have been Tony's fault? He was shaking and fairly drunk.

It must have taken a considerable amount of courage to walk to the inspector's office. As he approached, he would have smelled the aroma of percolating coffee and cigars which the father of his recent conquest used in large quantities. He would also have been monumentally relieved when he found out that he had submitted a seriously late court file. The Detective Inspector had no idea what had gone on, he didn't even know about the bar being closed. Tony had escaped.

Not long after this incident Tony and I ended up living in the same house. I rented the attic floor; Tony had a bed sitting room on the middle floor and the landlord lived on the ground floor. It should have been a comfortable set up but in reality, it became a bit of a nightmare.

Tony had three loves. His work, sex and alcohol, not necessarily in that order. The combination of these three things irritated and eventually infuriated our landlord, a man named Ted. Tony arrived home from work at all hours, often with women and almost invariably drunk. If he had been quiet then he could have got away with most things but Tony did not seem to do quiet.

I had only been in the house a couple of weeks and had come home from work about midnight and gone straight to bed. A couple of hours later Ted was banging on my door and when I opened it, he was in a highly agitated state. Water was poring through the ceiling of his living room which was directly underneath the bathroom I shared with Tony. The door to the bathroom was shut and there was no sign of Tony.

Ted and I decided we must open the bathroom door and, not without causing considerable damage, we managed to get it open. Tony was asleep in the bath still in his suit and with the tap still running. We dragged him out of the water and onto the floor. Slowly he came round and said he could remember thinking a bath would sober him up. Ted was incensed and I had an enormous amount of sympathy with him. Tony paid for the damage but the neither his near death by drowning experience nor the cost seemed to change his behaviour.

The Detective Inspector's daughter was a regular nocturnal visitor and she was obviously an enthusiastic and noisy sexual partner. As soon as the loved-up couple got into gear Ted would start banging on my door. Why he did not bang on Tony's door I never did find out. It was as if I was some sort of guardian for my drunken colleague. However, it was not a sexual partner that caused Tony to be given his notice, it was a fellow male police officer.

George Geddis was a tall, heavily built, lumbering sort of man. I found him very strange but Tony adopted George in the same way I had had to adopt Tony. He moved into a flat within a hundred meters of our house and he regularly came round to be fed or to sponge Polish Vodka off Tony. Eventually he offered to reciprocate and promised that he was going to cook us steak and chips.

The plan was that George would do the cooking and then ring us when it was ready. We waited and waited. It got to the stage that I really wanted to eat so Tony decided to go and see what was happening round the corner. He returned with bad news. George was at the Hospital and his flat was on fire, or rather it had been on fire but was now under several inches of water that had been used by the Fire Brigade to put the fire out.

George had bought the steak and vegetables, together with a bottle of whisky. Then, when he returned home, he realised he only had one pan and an oven tray. Not to be put off he cello taped a plate across the middle of the pan so he could cook potatoes and vegetables together and then placed the steak in the oven tray. Both pan and oven tray were placed on the electric hob and George poured himself a whisky.

He must have poured himself several whiskies because he never noticed the bottom burn out of the oven tray and the flames from the fat that the steaks were cooking in spread to the curtains and the polystyrene ceiling tiles. Fortunately, the room had a smoke alarm and, though George was unconscious through smoke or alcohol ingestion, he was saved.

That night George shared Tony's single bedded room. I was really happy knowing that of the occupants of the room below one had flooded a house and the other had nearly burned one down. That both were police officers came as no consolation whatsoever.

In the middle of the night Ted was banging at my door. He told me Tony had another lady friend staying and the screams were keeping him awake. I put my dressing gown on and went downstairs, unusually the door was ajar. As I looked inside Tony was standing on his bed looking genuinely scared and a sheet was floating round the room emitting wailing noises.

The reality was that George had been unable to sleep and had got bored so he decided to wake Tony, not like any normal person would have done but by wrapping a sheet round himself and moaning in his ear. Tony, half-drunk as usual, forgot

George was staying and thought he was being haunted. Ted gave George one night and Tony one week to vacate the house. Things were never the same for me again, thank goodness.

Tony and George continued to have the sort of adventures that would warrant a sitcom though it would be one with a dark side. Tony continued to drink heavily and to womanise seriously. One evening while attending a CID party he decided to photocopy some rugby songs. While attending an office with a photocopier he decided to fondle the breasts of a radio operator. She took exception to this and her supervisor became involved. Tony was suspended. All sorts of allegations and counter allegations flowed backwards and forwards but, in the end, Tony was severely reprimanded but kept his job (an unlikely outcome nowadays!). Matters could have been allowed to quieten down but the CID decided to have another party to welcome him back and during the festivities a senior detective presented my former flatmate with a large, carved, wooden breast.

News of the event made its way to the Chief Constable, more reprimands flowed and Tony eventually found himself posted far away from the scene of his offending. He settled down but found himself threatened by a criminal who he had arrested. The threats became more serious and though it could not be proved who was sending them Tony did not feel the job was protecting him. He resigned.

Unlike Tony, George was not a competent police officer. He also eventually got married but he continued to have scrapes that were largely unnecessary. The precise details and sequence of those scrapes have become a little shrouded in the mists of time but the gist remains true.

Living in a suburban area on the edge of the countryside George had a house that bordered a farmer's field. One day a sheep got stuck in the hedge that formed the border and gradually found itself half in and half out of George's Garden. Most people would have released the sheep or called the nearest farmer, few would have done what George did. He shot the sheep, he hung it in his garage and subsequently cut it up into joints for his freezer.

His next trick was to crash a police car. No surprise there you might think. Police officers have accidents just the same as any other motorist. George was driving back to the station when he went to sleep taking a corner, his car slid sideways into a wall. When he woke up the car was still running one side was almost flat from its impact with the wall the other side was completely undamaged.

If George had parked up at the scene of the accident, he would probably have been OK. A sergeant would have attended, he would have been breathalysed, suspended from driving and interviewed. Later he would have been reinstated and a decision would have been made whether or not he would face charges for careless or negligent driving. He would almost certainly have kept his job.

Instead of following the procedure outlined above George drove the car back to the station yard and parked the damaged side up against a wall. He signed the logbook to say the vehicle was in good condition and then he went home. Fortunately for the driver who was taking over from George he checked the car before getting in it. George had compounded the situation he had found himself in. He had left the scene of an accident and failed to report an accident. He had also, in all probability, falsified a police document. He was in the mire!

That George survived says a lot about how difficult it was then to recruit police officers. Like Tony he was posted a long way from the scene of his accident but even then, his strange behaviour did not stop. He had always been hard up, drink and gambling being the most likely culprits for that state of affairs, and he was always looking for ways of supplementing his pay. One opportunity cropped up when he came into possession of a small amount of seafood. He sold it to his colleagues at work and they were so impressed they clamoured for more.

George, never one to let the chance of money slip him by secured an extra supply of mussels. He sold several bags of them even though most people would have preferred the prawns of his first delivery. Over the next few days several of the purchasers went sick, all of them with cases of sickness and diarrhoea. All of them blamed the mussels and a traffic officer later told me that George had got them off a sewage outfall pipe in a local estuary.

I am sure that if anyone ever reads this book some may think that it is always the junior ranks who get tarred with the brush of drink related idiocy. Hopefully I shall put that right when I move on to my time at the Police Staff College but I was becoming aware of the fact that alcohol did not recognize rank boundaries even then.

My first Chief Constable, a man I still hold in high regard, was an accomplished musician and a strong supporter of the Police Force Band. He was also a fairly strait-laced family man with a strong sense of keeping up appearances. During his leadership of the Force a tradition was renewed that saw senior officers meet together and dine at a number of the more exclusive restaurants in the Force area. These events were very proper and the after-dinner speakers were selected from the ranks of the judiciary, landed gentry or other such.

One of these events was held in a large rambling establishment which had a public bar as well as the usual restaurant. A local lawyer had finished his talk and some of the officers dispersed to the bar. There a number of them got talking to a small group of women who were quickly recognized as sex workers from the local red-light area. Rather than admit to being off duty police officers someone hit upon the bright idea of saying that they were a male voice choir who had been performing locally.

That and the large amounts of booze they were plied with relaxed the ladies and the evening progressed. After some time, the Chief Constable came to find his lost senior management and walked in upon them at play with the ladies. He was introduced as the Choirmaster and the ladies were described as dancers. For the next hour the Chief talked music while some of those there drunkenly haggled for a cheap rate knee trembler. It is fortunate for all that the photographer who had taken pictures for the Force magazine had left before the choir met the dancers!

Finally, for now, I will introduce you to a character who appears later. One particular Deputy Chief Constable that I worked with/for was a particular drip. He was a chinless specimen with a shock of thinning and unruly fair hair. This individual originated in a county to the north of my Force and initially knew little of the local geography. To help him settle in he was taken to an old-world pub in a small town about ten miles from the city. This pub, one of the oldest in England, served its beer from jugs, the floors were tiled, the ceilings beamed and the lights provided by gas.

After several pints of the famous local brew the new arrival stated that he did not believe that the lights were gas powered. Assurances that they were fell on deaf ears. He stood up, walked to a vacant seat under a wall light and looked down into the glowing glass bowl. Briefly he may have seen the white-hot gas mantle, just before his fringe caught fire and he fell back off the chair. Not an auspicious start in a new Force and yet again it was in a pub and alcohol was involved!

When Tony was disciplined for his improper behaviour he faced working at a new station, this coincided with Ted asking him to leave his bed sitting room. In a strange way the situation unsettled me. I had got into a rut of going to work, arresting a drunk or a shoplifter and going home again. The problem was that I felt like I was waiting to go on the Bramshill Course that I had been selected for. Everything felt like marking time and nobody seemed willing to take me on a more permanent basis. Everything I did seemed to be on the understanding that I would not be there long.

Effectively, that is exactly what the superintendent said when I asked for an extended posting to the CID. Why, he asked, should he train me to do a job when as soon as I was competent, I would be off to Bramshill and never work for him again. I tried to argue that it would be over a year before I left for the course but the decision to leave me where I was had clearly been made.

I decided to do something about it but could not think what. Then a vacancy was advertised in another Division of the Force. A rural beat officer was required to police a number of small hamlets to the north of the city. The post holder would be required to live in a police house on the beat and be available to meet the needs of the local community whenever they arose. The attractions for me were that the work would be different to what I was doing, I would be my own boss most of the time and I would not have to live in a flat.

I did not really spend much time thinking about what the negatives of taking the post might be. Fortunately, the man who interviewed me sat back and took a much broader look at the situation than I had. He told me that I had received glowing reports from my existing supervisors who all thought I would be a competent rural officer. However, rural communities, he said, required continuity and they did not like change. I might be the best beat officer they had ever had but in just over a year there would be a vacancy again. Further, he asked me if I really thought policing in the city had prepared me for a rural beat. Where would I take a prisoner if I arrested at midnight and the nearest of my colleagues was twenty miles away? How many shotgun applications had I looked at? How many school talks had I given? He went on and on and I realized my experience was extremely limited.

It was starting to feel like a 'Catch 22' situation. I was working in a job where I had exhausted the learning opportunities but no one would let me do anything else because I had no experience. Then he told me that he admired the fact that I was trying to broaden my knowledge and that he would help if he could. He would not, however, be taking me on as one of his rural beat officers.

A week later I was called to the office of my own superintendent and told that I was being posted to another station. He spoke as if he could not understand why anyone would want to leave the city centre to police in a backwater but told me that I was going anyway! Three days later I went.

I like to think that the kindly superintendent who interviewed me had intervened on my behalf but in reality, I have no idea what happened. I had enjoyed working in the city, after years of going from one job to another I felt I had settled down. When I left Bramshill, having completed my year long Accelerated Promotion Course, I was posted back to the city. I was quietly pleased when I received the notification, however, it was to be a very different experience when I returned.

CHAPTER ELEVEN

GREAT DAYS

My new station was only some five miles out of the city but it may as well have been on a different planet. To the east was the suburban sprawl of the city itself but to the west was a large rural area that stretched for over twenty miles. There were three or four large villages and a market town, but for the most part the population was sparsely spread.

The station itself was an old house to which had been added newer extensions and outbuildings. Everything was crammed because the main building had never been designed to hold the levels of staffing that were now required. There were, however, cells, interview rooms, a control room, a snooker room and a multiplicity of one desked offices.

When I arrived for duty on my first night, I was told that I should have reported to a 'Police Box' some six or seven miles away. The box, named imaginatively Bristol Street after the street on which it stood, was a brick-built building. There was a room for writing reports and eating refreshments, a room for meeting members of the public and a toilet. It was a very basic construction but I was to spend many happy shifts working from there.

The delights of Bristol Street were to be denied me on my first night. The control room was short of staff. It did not seem to matter as I pointed out I had never worked in a control room. There was it seemed a first time for everything. I felt completely lost as I tried to work out which wire went where and which button then needed pressing to connect phones or answer radios. After about an hour the sergeant left the room, he was followed by the only other constable and then finally the civilian radio operator also went. I was all alone.

I am sure I sent the wrong officers to the wrong places on numerous occasions that night and I certainly disconnected lots of people who were trying to ring the station. Strangely, though, no one seemed to bother all that much and bit by bit I started to get the hang of it. Indeed, the most worrying thing was that none of the people who had left the room came back again and there was a powerful smell of burning coming from somewhere on the station.

At last, absolutely desperate for the toilet, I also left the control room and made my way to the parade/refreshment room. The police constable who had been on duty in the control room was fast asleep and snoring gently. The sergeant and the civilian were huddled over the gas hob and I quickly realized that was where the smell was coming from. They were melting small ingots of lead in a milk pan and pouring the liquid metal into moulds on the work surface next to the sink.

The sergeant explained to me that he was making split shot and weights for fishing. Further, it had to be done there and then because they were going fishing straight from work. All three of the control room staff came back into the radio room twenty minutes before the end of the shift. There followed a frenetic writing up of occurrence sheets and reports outlining the events of the night and then fishing tackle was loaded up and off they went for the real business of the day!

The second night of my new posting I reported to Bristol Street, where I was handed the keys of a patrol car. There was no briefing as such, no sergeant to tell us what we were to do as there had been in the city. Instead, a copious quantity of Chinese food was distributed to each of us. This had been provided by the local Chinese takeaway and it took nearly an hour to eat everything that was on the table.

I then drove out onto the streets. This was the first time I had driven a marked police car since I terrified the doctor and it was a strange experience, though one which I could not think about for long. I quickly received a report of two men fighting in the street near a well-known public toilet. I arrived quickly and there rolling around on the wet road surface were two strange looking individuals. One of them had a comb over hairstyle and during the skirmish this had become dishevelled and hung down one side of his head revealing a large bald area. The other man was wearing an olive-coloured raincoat and he had curly black hair brushed back off his face. 'Mr. Comb Over' was wearing pink, flared trousers and Cuban heeled shoes; his paisley pattern shirt was open to his waist.

In spite of their strange appearance the two men were exchanging some quite formidable blows, so I immediately tried to drag them apart. Another patrol car arrived and we arrested the men for breaching the peace. We conveyed them both to the station where the control sergeant I had worked with the night before received them in the custody office.

It transpired that the man in the raincoat was a well-known local rough sleeper who spent any money that came his way on cider. On this night he had sought refuge from the rain in the toilets. There he had selected a cubicle, opened his cider and sat happily reading a sports newspaper. Mr 'Comb Over' had gone to the toilets for very different reasons. He had gone in the cubicle next to the raincoat wearer and he had quickly seen that there was a hole cut in the partition wall between the two cubicles. As individuals of his type were prone to do, he pushed his penis through the hole and into the adjacent cubicle. This may well have been an invitation to some sort of sexual activity but it did not impress the man next door. He looked at the end of the protruding penis and obviously concluded it was a good place to extinguish his cigarette. From this point the fight was inevitable.

Both men were out of the station and back into the night within minutes of their arrival in front of the sergeant. My protestations that there was some sort of sexual offence that should be explored fell on stony ground. The breach of the peace was over, it was not likely to recur and the men had, therefore, been advised about their future conduct. This may have been pragmatic but it was not the way we had done things in the city. The learning experience I had wanted had clearly begun!

Most of the time I got on with my control room sergeant very well and he regularly sought me out to stand in for absences among his regular staff. However, it was not long after the 'battle of the toilets' that I tested his patience again. This time it had a real impact on his preparations for fishing.

One Saturday evening I found myself working a rural beat and was sitting in a patrol car in what seemed like the middle of nowhere. I had the car heater turned up full and did not feel like doing much at all. Meanwhile in the city a football match had taken place between the local team and Burnley. I remembered Burnley when, in the 1960's, they had been a team to be reckoned with. They, like our local team, had fallen on hard times, though they still had a fair-sized fan base.

On this particular Saturday a group of Burnley supporters had travelled to the match in a Ford Transit van. The vehicle was a wreck and its appearance had not been enhanced by someone having painted the slogan "Inham's Guerrillas" down the side. Somehow thirteen people had crammed into this vehicle when it departed from the local football ground and nearly an hour later, they all disembarked in a sleepy little village on my temporary beat.

On the face of it the stop was a peaceful one, they wanted food and toilets and there was little chance of them finding rival supporters in the village. Sadly, there were no toilets so one or two of Burnley's finest began to relieve themselves in a garden. Others made their way to the local fish and chip shop while a further group knocked on a door and asked to use the house toilet. From this point things went badly wrong. A fight broke out in the fish shop over who had ordered the last piece of Cod, the unwanted visitors who went looking for a toilet were refused entry but forced their way in and urinated in the hallway, while those who used a garden as a toilet broke the wall down when trying to get back to their van.

Within minutes the phone lines in the control room were blocked by reports of what was going on. I was sent to check matters out and there was a promise that backup would be sent if needed. When I arrived, the hostilities were over. Rubble from the damaged wall lay on the footpath, a distraught householder was being helped by neighbours as she mopped up urine from her hall floor and the chip shop proprietor was closing for the night. This was the most significant thing to have happened in the village for years and they wanted action not a single constable offering to take statements.

I made a speedy decision to see if I could catch the transit van before it left the area covered by my Force. My police car whined and wheezed as I flogged it to its' maximum speed but there was no sign of the vehicle I was looking for. Each mile that I covered took me nearer the Force boundary and the stretch of Motorway that led to it. I was not supposed to go on the Motorway in a patrol car as I had not the equipment or training to deal with the things that happened there.

As the Motorway loomed ever nearer, I saw the tail lights of the transit and I tried to radio for assistance. I received no reply and realized that I was probably in a radio black spot or at the very edge reception. One thing was certain, I was not going to let the culprits escape when I was so close to them. As they joined the Motorway, so did I. The patrol car I was driving had a blue light, which I switched on, but it had no two-tone horns. I found it difficult to get passed the transit to stop it.

Eventually, with less than a hundred meters to go before entering the neighbouring Force area I caused the driver stop. Only then did it start to dawn on me just how many of them there were. It seemed like a continuous flow of humanity as one after another Burnley supporter disembarked onto the hard shoulder. They lined up sheepishly and surprisingly quietly until it started to dawn that there were thirteen of them and only one of me. I took the keys out of the ignition of the transit and looked in the back. There, in the middle of the van was a park bench strapped to the floor with pieces of rope that disappeared through rust holes in the body work to unseen anchor points.

As I tried again to contact control, the supporters started to become restless and two of them ran off down an embankment at the side of the road. I still had eleven and to my relief a Traffic Patrol car pulled up. There were now two of us but more importantly the traffic car had a Force radio and was able to ensure back up was despatched.

Just before a van arrived to convey my new prisoners to the station, the missing two returned. They had fallen in a drainage ditch and were absolutely soaked and covered in clayey mud. Thus, it was that all thirteen arrived in front of my control room sergeant. He was not a happy Chappy!

Eventually two of them were charged with damaging the wall, two were charged with damage in the fish and chip shop and all were charged with public order offences. The paperwork took me hours but the traffic officer really went to town with the driver and the vehicle. I cannot remember the precise number of offences but they included operating as a public service vehicle(bus), driving without a licence, without insurance, without an MOT and literally dozens of offences relating to the safety of the vehicle.

I thought it had been a successful operation, albeit I was lucky to have stopped them when I did and even luckier not to have been thrown down the embankment. My control sergeant was not convinced. I had displayed more of those worrying city ways which would cause me problems in the future. I had also delayed an evening of making lead shot for a fishing trip. Some things are unforgivable.

My new station might have been housed in a building from another age but it had a secret weapon that I never found anywhere else. The cell block would not have been out of place in the dungeons of a medieval castle. The four cells had low arched doorways and vaulted ceilings. Light in the corridor leading to the cells was extremely low and in the cells themselves it was always dark.

One afternoon I was sent to collect a shoplifter from the local Boots' store and although the individual was loaded down with cosmetic items, he would not admit having to having taken them from Boots. The station sergeant was adamant that I must get the prisoner to say that the goods came from Boots so that he could draft the appropriate charge. I asked and asked again but without the desired admission being forthcoming. At last, the sergeant told me to go and get 'Big Tom'.

Leaving the shoplifter sitting in the dingy cell block I went to find the secret weapon. Tom Kennedy was a detective in the sub divisional CID. He was a mild tempered man with thinning fair hair, but his main attribute was that he was huge. I am over six feet tall and built like a rugby player, but Tom was at least two of me.

I found him sitting at a typewriter and, though clearly busy, he willingly came with me to cell block. On arrival there he told me to tell the prisoner that he was coming and to dim the light in the cell. I did as I was told and I could sense the change in the shoplifter. Tom walked towards the cell and turned sideways and stooped so he could get through the door. I was inside with the prisoner and as Tom manoeuvred himself in, the light behind him was completely blocked. The cell was in total darkness and all I could hear was a voice shouting, "Everything came from Boots."

Every time a prisoner was being troublesome or uncooperative Big Tom was called and seldom did he fail to inspire the correct result. Years later the Police and Criminal Evidence Act restricted many police practices but I think Big Tom would still have been legal.

Most days passed without undue excitement but we did a lot of jobs that today's police officers would never do. Each beat had a number of addresses that we called at to help elderly or infirm occupants get in or out of bed. I have also done the shopping for some people who had no one else. We also used to collect prisoners' meals from an old people's home until an arsonist burned it down. I was very happy until a new patrol sergeant arrived.

My first run in with him was completely unnecessary. As I was leaving Bristol Street Box a collision took place at the nearby traffic lights. A police officer was standing nearby and it was obvious that she should deal with the situation. I stopped to see if I could offer any help but as I got out of the car I was called to another job. The female constable asked what she should do as the driver of the offending vehicle said it was not his car. I quickly told her that if the car was stolen, she should ask for assistance and arrest the driver. If the car was not his, but he had been given permission to drive it, then the question would be whether or not he was insured. She seemed happy and after we checked that the vehicle was not stolen, I left her to it.

Several hours later the new sergeant approached me as I was eating my sandwiches at the station. He immediately accused me of telling the constable to arrest the driver for having no insurance. There was no way I could convince him that I had said no such thing and months later he criticized me in an annual appraisal for lack of legal knowledge. It seemed so unjust but matters were to get worse.

The other outside sergeant was a man who I regarded as a friend, we had played rugby together and I shall mention him again later. One evening he called me to say that the new sergeant, who was diabetic, had left his insulin at home and I was to collect it immediately. I set off to do this but about half way there I received another radio message from the same sergeant telling me to attend a disturbance at an address en route. I found no disturbance at the house I had been sent to and set off again for the insulin. Again, I received a message this time sending me to a suspected break in at a shop. Once again nothing seemed to be happening and I resumed. This happened on another occasion and when I arrived at the sergeants' home his wife was almost hysterical with anxiety.

Back at the station the sergeant was clearly not well, he was sweating and was a sallow grey colour. My 'friend' standing in as control room sergeant thought the situation was hilarious. When I checked the Occurrence Sheets later, not one of the jobs I had been sent to was reported! I had been set up by someone else who did not like my antagonist.

Later, I again became the pawn in the ongoing hostilities between my two sergeants. It was a bitterly cold night and for some reason the Councils' gritting lorries did not seem to be in action. In the market town that housed my station there was a central square with a narrow road running round it's sides. This road came to resemble a skating rink and vehicles were slipping and sliding as they negotiated the corners.

After a collision had taken place in the square I was called to the station and there my least favourite sergeant was waiting for me. I was told to empty all the equipment out of my patrol car and fill the boot with road grit from a store nearby. I was then to take the grit and spread it round the square. I did not think that I should be doing this but I had learned not to question his instructions.

As I worked away shovelling grit on the corners of the square, I noticed the other sergeant arrive. He walked up to me and asked what on earth I was doing. As I explained my instructions, he seemed less than pleased. He pointed out that the grit would rot the metal of the car boot and that if we had rung the Council's emergency number, they would have turned out to do what was their job. His final message to me was that I should empty out the last of the grit, wash out the boot of the car and get some real police work done.

As I hosed out the boot the first sergeant arrived and asked if I had finished gritting the square. I referred him to the second sergeant and left them to sort it out. They were like chalk and cheese. One was a career traffic officer who did things by the book, the other had been promoted from the Regional Crime Squad and did not seem to know what the book was.

The sergeant from the crime background had lived a charmed life as a police officer. On one occasion he had been working with the Crime Squad and the days' work had ended with a boozy session in a number of pubs and clubs across the north of England. He had been driving the unmarked Police car which was a top of the range BMW and he dropped off his colleagues before heading home.

The next morning, he woke late. His wife had already departed for work and the children were at school. He showered, dressed and went to get in the BMW that he was sure he had driven home in. There was no car in his garage and none on the road outside his house. He rang work and asked if the BMW was parked there but was informed it was not. The minutes of the clock ticked by as he drank coffee and tried to remember what had actually happened the night before.

At last, he rang a colleague and asked for a lift to work and when he heard a vehicle pull up outside his house, he made his way out for his lift. There, on the footpath stood his neighbour looking perplexed. Then the sergeant noticed that the garage next door was open and in it neatly parked was the BMW. In his drunken stupor he parked in the wrong garage. He was saved embarrassment at work by the narrowest of margins.

A little after that incident I went on rugby tour to Belfast with a group which included the forgetful driver. After a day's drinking and a hard match against the Royal Ulster Constabulary we ended up heading for our hotel on a large coach. We stopped for some food to soak up the alcohol and I bought a whole Family Size Bucket of Kentucky Fried

Chicken. As I got back on the bus and walked past what I thought was the comatose sergeant, a huge hand flew out and grabbed a handful of my food.

Twenty minutes later we pulled up outside the hotel and numerous dishevelled individuals started to disembark. One or two were now fast asleep on the coach so we went to wake them. The thief of my food did not look well, he was a strange colour but most significantly he seemed to be foaming at the mouth! A doctor was called by the RUC man who was chaperoning us but before he arrived it became obvious what had happened. The handful from my bucket that the sergeant had eaten contained four scented hand towels as well as several portions of fries. The foaming was explained.

CHAPTER TWELVE

BEWARE OF ANIMALS

One thing I learned quite early at my new station was that I should keep away from animals. The southern border of my new sub division was a large river and it was to the banks of the river that I was called one midweek evening.

The river flowed into a tidal estuary and at the time I arrived it was low tide. The lady who had called the Police was standing next to a car on a piece of parkland. She came running over to me as I parked my patrol car.

"I think he's dead." She told me while pointing vaguely in the direction of the river.

"Who's dead?' I asked.

"He's out there, in the mud. He's probably fallen off a boat or topped himself"

I peered out at the river. I could see about thirty or forty meters of thick, shiny mud and beyond that a channel in which the river was flowing quite quickly. I could not see a body of any description. Sensing that this was the case, the woman grasped my arm and pulled me nearer to the mud while pointing with her other arm. Finally, I could make out a shadowy outline that could have been a body or perhaps a log!

Another car pulled up and then yet another, clearly, I had not been the only assistance that the woman had called. The growing crowd all agreed that they could see a body, some said the outline was the head and shoulders of a young man. What was clear, even to me, was that the tide was coming in. It was also obvious that there was no way of getting across the thick glutinous mud.

In the back of the car, I had a length of rope with a flotation aid attached. The aid was unlikely to be of any use as the 'body' had not moved since my arrival and I assumed we were dealing with a corpse. I did, however, have a grappling hook for dragging vehicles out of ditches. The hook quickly replaced the flotation aid and I squelched as far into the mud as I felt was safe.

I swung the rope round my head, narrowly missing some of the onlookers, and let it sail out over the mud. The hook landed with a plop in the mud several feet away from the body. I tried again with the same result. As I tried a third time, I heard mumblings that I could hurt the person we were trying to rescue. A moments panic gripped me as the rope and hook flew out over the mud. Then there was a sickening noise as the prongs of the hook thudded into flesh.

I pulled on the rope and the body started to slip across the mud. It was heavy and I had to tug hard but as it came nearer, I could make out the colour of skin. The woman who had made the call to the Police collapsed behind me and I am sure I heard someone being sick. Then to my relief I realized I had not impaled a living human. The object in the mud was a full-grown sow. I pulled it in and sat back on the bonnet of my patrol car.

Someone much brighter than me in the control room called a vet and he arrived quickly from a local surgery. The pig had no identifiable markings but did have blisters on its trotters, which I was told could indicate swine vascular disease. I was pleased to see the back of it!

Within days I was back at the river or rather back at an almost complete bridge that was being built across the river. The centre span had yet to be added but approach roads and signage were all in place.

Someone had reported that a horse had escaped from a nearby field and was walking on the bridge. I parked away from the bridge and got my trusted rope from the boot of the patrol car then set out to find the horse. It was exactly where it was reported as being. I walked towards it slowly trying not to reveal my fear of horses and things went very well. The horse did not run away, it stood perfectly still as I tried to fashion a noose that I could place round its neck to lead it off the bridge.

The rope in place, I set off with my equine friend who trotted behind like a dog on a lead. Then the cavalry arrived in the form of a traffic patrol car with its blue lights flashing and horns blaring. It was like flicking a switch. My well-behaved horse became a demented lump of hurtling muscle, racing back towards the gap in the middle of the bridge. I was dragged along behind like a rag doll, the rope twisted round my wrist.

I remember my left boot coming off and things going into slow motion. The stars were shining and I actually wondered if I could survive the fall into the waters below. Then the horse stopped only feet from the edge and it stood snorting as I tried to get up. The traffic officer approached sheepishly from the safe end of the bridge.

"You shouldn't tie yourself to them!" He said.

I could have killed him but I gave him the horse as I went back to retrieve my boot.

I then managed to avoid animals for a good while, if you don't count the police dog that was sick over my best shoes. However, I might as well tell you my other animal stories here though they are out of sequence.

As an inspector I became Staff Officer to the Chief Constable. I will explain what that entailed later, but for now it suffices that on occasion I drove the Chief to places or events he wanted to attend. One morning I had been to the local hospital for the results of some allergy tests. As the nurse removed a series of strips that had been attached to my back, she informed me that I appeared to be allergic to the household dust mite, rye pollen, horse hair and cats. Taking the correct tablets should control the symptoms, she told me.

When I returned to my office the Chief wanted to be driven half way across the Force area to a Division I was not really familiar with. He sat in the back of the Jaguar as I tried to keep the gear changes smooth and as my confidence grew, I asked where we were going. The answer was almost unbelievable.

Several lions had escaped from a circus in the middle of a fairly large town. Police officers using riot shields and dustbin lids had cornered them and marched them back to the circus. We were going to see the lions and the officers. Not only did this remind me of my father but it meant that I would be in a tent with lions only hours after having been told I was allergic to cats. It could only happen to me.

The final story to tell you about in this group involves me more directly. I have noticed nowadays that the presenters of naturalist documentaries tend to call fish animals. I have never been convinced by that but it does allow me to tell the story here.

I was working at a town with a small port that imported wood, cars and foodstuffs including fish. The town was run down with many commercial premises being closed and boarded up. Early in my time at this particular station I had been driving along a dual carriageway when, in a telephone box at the other side of the road, I thought I saw a slumped figure. I had to drive two or three miles before I could turn round and so I asked the control to send another patrol.

There was no body. I must have seen a shadow and it caused much levity among the constables on my relief. I was determined to be careful in the future.

One night, I was sat in my patrol car at the side of some traffic lights that controlled a junction leading to the port. It was well past midnight and there was hardly a vehicle on the roads. From my position I could see a considerable distance in three directions, only to the rear did I have a blind spot. The car was warm and I was thinking how nice it would feel to be in bed. Then from behind me I heard a noise or probably sensed a movement. A bicycle passed my position and failed to stop at the red traffic light in its path.

It was not the bicycle or the fact it had committed an offence that attracted my attention, rather it was the rider of the cycle. This was one I definitely could not radio in. The cycle was ridden by a fish!

I was initially so stunned that the fish cycled nearly two hundred meters before I set off in pursuit. It wobbled once or twice but for the most part followed a straight course on the correct side of the road. I switched the blue lights of my vehicle on, more to warn any other road users than to stop the fish. After half a mile I decided enough was enough and pulled alongside the piscine cyclist.

The cycle did not slow down but the scaly rider seemed to turn sideways to look at me. Momentarily I saw legs coming from the abdomen of the fish and then the cycle and rider wobbled again and fell to the floor. I parked my car, left the blue light flashing and made my way to the struggling heap in the roadway. There I found a small Irishman extricating himself from the insides of a large Cod. He had a woolly hat on his head and he had literally been wearing the fish, having put the fish head and gills over his head and wrapping the rest of the disembowelled fish round his torso.

The Irishman was drunk but he was able to give me an account of what led him to be cycling, dressed as a fish, in the middle of the night. Apparently, he had been drinking with some Icelandic sailors and they had invited him back to their ship for a game of cards. His winnings were converted into the fish and the only way he could get it home was on his bicycle.

I arrested him for being drunk in charge of a pedal cycle and as I write this now, I think what a rotten thing that was to do. However, at the time I had no way of checking his story, he had been wobbling about the roadway, he had ignored a red light on a main road and he had eventually fallen off the bike. If anything happened to him, I would be responsible. So, at the time it seemed the only thing to do and he, his bike and the large fish were conveyed to the station.

I completed the paperwork while the cyclist snored happily in a drunk cell and then went home to dream of being chased by giant fish round the local streets.

It was two days before I was next at work and when I arrived, I was not popular! The station stank of fish. I had asked that the fish be photographed and disposed of but someone had booked it into the property store in my name. No one wanted to countermand the inspector, so the fish sat there next to radiator slowly cooking and decomposing. I was glad that I had the liberty to go out on patrol and the authority to blame someone else for the smell!

Anyway, all these animal stories have been a digression I was still a constable at my new station and mostly happy with the way things were going. Then out of the blue I was told I was being transferred to Traffic. To this day I do not know who decided this would be a good idea. I was, at best, an average driver; I had shown no real interest in being a Traffic Officer and one of my sergeants would doubt I had the knowledge to do the job. I was keen to avoid the posting but I had no idea how to go about it.

I was informed that I was to be given a test drive in a Traffic Car by one of the Force's top instructors and examiners. This individual, Larry Holmes, was a complex character. He had the facial appearance of a professional prize fighter and huge hands to match, yet he could regularly be heard playing classical music on the piano at Divisional Headquarters.

Larry did not suffer fools gladly and was known to 'explode' if provoked but I had always found him a reasonable and likeable man. On the day of the test, he arrived punctually and took his place in the front passenger seat. He instructed me to drive towards the Force boundary and for twenty minutes or so we had a pleasant trip in spring sunshine. It was almost idyllic and only spoiled by his occasionally asking me to commentate on my driving.

After a time, he seemed totally relaxed and asked why I wanted to go in Traffic. I was honest in my reply, telling him that I had no desire to leave my current posting and that I would have preferred CID if I had to go anywhere.

"Well, if that's the case you better do something about it, 'cos in five minutes I'm going to tell you you've passed and you are going to be a Traffic Man."

The grey matter stirred slowly as I realized he needed some evidence to fail me as a suitable driver for the Traffic Department. Was I willing to take the risk that by failing I might end up having to be retested to drive any police vehicles? What could I do? The whole trip had gone well? Then a pheasant stepped out of the ferns at the side of the road and I swerved across the road to avoid it.

"I think that will do," said Larry. "You are clearly unsuited for Traffic duties."

That was it. Larry was good as his word. My least favourite sergeant thought it was hilarious and one or two friends said they were pleased I would be staying where I was. The only thing is, I didn't. Within days I was posted to the CID and what an eye opener that was!

CHAPTER THIRTEEN

ACE DETECTIVE

Those who are joining the Police Service today would not recognise what used to pass as the Criminal Investigation Department. Indeed, there was a considerable degree of variation in structures between Forces in the days when I joined.

Basically, when I joined the CID, the Force had six Divisions and these were in turn divided into sub divisions. My station was the sub divisional headquarters, three miles down a road from the divisional headquarters and five miles along a different road from Force Headquarters. The sub division had a Detective Chief Inspector, two detective inspectors, four detective sergeants and four teams of between four and six detective constables. At Division there was a detective superintendent, two detective Chief Inspectors and a small Divisional team of detectives. Headquarters had a Detective Chief Superintendent, two detective superintendents, two detective chief inspectors and a number of officers of various ranks filling specialist posts in, for example, the Scenes of Crime Unit or Special Branch etc.

I was joining at the lowest level, a detective constable in a sub divisional team. However, being in the CID carried a certain status. Some members of the public still think that becoming a detective is some form of promotion out of uniform ranks. Some members of the criminal fraternity would only talk to detectives as they felt this signified that they had a certain status themselves. Thus "Plod" or the "Woodentops" were names given to uniform officers who had to be kept well away from real police work......Crime.

The whole situation was an illusion. I knew no more, was no more capable or in any way shrewder after I joined the CID than I was before. Uniform officers often caught the real villains, such as Peter Sutcliffe, they were just not allowed to interview them or do the paperwork afterwards.

It is amazing that some detectives managed to preserve any sort of aura of professionalism. Many of them were 'paper shufflers.' When a crime was reported by a member of the public a uniform officer would visit and record the basic details on a Crime Report. The uniform officer was supposed to do a few basic inquiries and then pass the report to the CID. After a degree of administrative recording and checking, the reports were allocated for 'investigation'.

The investigation might only involve a phone call being made to the victim, though most people did receive a visit by a detective. Bureaucracy then took over because the officers received more reports than they could manage and their main objective was to get rid of them.

This process of 'getting rid' could only be managed if a detective inspector signed the report off as a case where there had never been a crime or all meaningful enquiries had been completed. It could be as difficult to get a crime report written off as it was to find the perpetrator of the crime. Detectives became adept at what they had to write on the reports to satisfy a D/I(inspector). However, some officers accumulated vast numbers of reports that they could not get rid of and which they had little chance of ever detecting.

One detective I worked with was regarded as a hardworking and capable individual. I quickly found that he spent most of his time pursuing women or selling things from the boot of his car. One day he was involved in a traffic collision, driving his own vehicle when off duty. When uniform officers arrived, he was being loaded into an ambulance. His car was a total write off with pieces of it strewn around a sharp bend. The most notable thing at the scene was the number of paper crime reports floating around in the air and collecting in trees and at the side of the road. Literally hundreds of reports were written off as no one but the detective knew what had been done with them and he was too badly injured to return to work for some time. I have heard that almost twenty percent of the stations outstanding crime reports were written off as having been lost in the accident. No one seemed to ask why an off-duty detective was carrying hundreds of crime reports around in the boot of his car? The answer was that he was a bone idle, lazy loafer who did not know what to do with them and after the crash several other bone idle, loafers got rid of their outstanding work by saying they had transferred their reports to the injured officer.

New officers were not immediately accepted as members of the close-knit detective fraternity. Thus, I found myself paired with another individual who had also just joined. We sat around the office waiting to be told what to do and were eventually told to get out and do something. So, we went out and wandered around aimlessly until we eventually saw two men pushing a pram.

One of the men was tall and black the other was shorter and stocky. The pram belonged with them, it was dirty, missing pieces and it had seen better days. It was filled with large lumps of rolled lead and the men said they had found it outside a pub. We arrested them on the basis that they had stolen the lead from someone. This was my first big CID job!

The threat of Big Tom did little to loosen the tongues of the supposed thieves. They said nothing and it took several attempts to get their real names. Both men were known villains and they had once been established professional criminals. Years of heavy drinking and old age had rendered them shadows of their past. I believed we had enough to charge them even without any confession, my colleague did not agree.

In those days, when interviewed, a suspect could make a statement or their answers would be recorded and used as evidence. Sat in the cell, talking to one of the men, my fellow rookie constable decided he would ask the questions and I would write down the answers.

"Where did you get the lead?" He asked'
There was no reply. My colleague turned to me and said,
"We nicked it off Wellbourne Street."
"I didn't say fuck all!" Said the man.
"Where were you taking the lead? "
"I'm saying nowt."
"Write down, 'we were taking it to a scrappy'(scrapyard)."
The man was becoming agitated. I wrote as I was told.

"This is fucking wrong," shouted the alleged offender.

"Write down. 'We are sorry we done it' ".

The man leapt at my colleague and together we had to restrain him. The interview was over. My fellow 'detective' left the cell block and I sat in the Custody Office waiting for him. While I did so our other prisoner asked to see me. He told me that the lead was from an old chapel and that they had already taken one load to a scrapyard quite near to where we had found them. He gave me a full statement.

Ten minutes later my absent colleague wandered back into the office.

"The D/I says we've enough to charge them". He looked genuinely pleased with himself.

"It's called verballing", he said. "I've read about it."

When I showed him the statement and the questions and answers that I had torn up he looked genuinely perplexed.

"Why have you done that?"

"Because it was wrong!" I said.

I never worked with him again and I was extremely pleased that I did not have to. Years later whilst off duty he was arrested on suspicion of arson. As far as I can remember he set fire to a club for payment from the owner. His lifestyle had been chaotic and he had been up to his neck in debt when he lit the fire. It convinced me that some people are dodgy all the time. I must, however, stress that I never saw anyone else use the "verballing" technique in an interview.

As I look back now on my time in CID it has a much darker aspect than I ever remember it having at the time. We always seemed to be shuffling reports and papers in a way that made rough edges smooth. The very nature of the people that CID officers deal with ensures that you are rarely told the whole truth and sometimes no truth at all. Yet to satisfy the requirements of justice the truth must be pursued and proved beyond reasonable doubt. Securing the truth created headaches and took a long time and even in those days there was not enough time. Now the Police ignore whole chunks of crime, they have given in. When I was in the CID, we tried to do everything and ended up being dissatisfied most of the time.

There were some lighter intervals. I remember on one crisp October morning being asked to accompany a detective sergeant. We were going to give advice to a householder about preventing intruders getting into her house. This was not strictly speaking CID work as the sub division had a Crime Prevention Officer who was a specialist in alarms, locks and the like.

As we approached the house, to which we were travelling, I could see why a detective sergeant had been sent. Tall walls surrounded a massive house. The gates were electric and there were security lights on the drive and walls. The only improvement I could see would have been to cut down one or two shrubs to improve angles of view from the house and that would not have been aesthetically acceptable.

The trees in the area were turning many shades of brown as they readied themselves to fall. The sun shone but the flowers and plants in the borders had that autumnal appearance of decay. We were met at the door of the house by a woman who looked as if she had just come back from the golf course, her face was flushed and her clothes made from an assortment of tweed cloth.

The sergeant I was accompanying was an experienced detective of many years service. He was something of a legend, a rough diamond but with an indefinable quality that was much valued, he was a "Thief Taker", a man who looked at a crime and immediately knew who had done it. I could see him looking round the modern kitchen to which we had been taken. There was every sort of labour-saving device known to man and nothing looked like it had ever been used. We were offered home-made lemonade, not the usual tea or coffee, and I got a frosty stare from my companion when I accepted.

"I understand that you are worried about intruders?" The sergeant began.

"I am officer. They are disgusting. I don't know what to do."

"What have you done up to now?" The sergeant continued.

"Well, I've kept the windows shut of course and the doors and I've used traps but they don't seem to work"

I detected a splutter as the sergeant heard this last comment.

"What sort of traps?" He asked.

"Oh! Just the usual sticky ones. I don't like to spray them".

The sergeant looked perplexed and I had no idea what she was talking about, but then he revealed the reason why he was already a sergeant.

"What sort of intruders are we talking about?"

"Flies," the lady said, "big black ones, like those on the window."

I then noticed two big, black bluebottles buzzing on the long kitchen window.

"So, you've rung the police to talk about flies?' The sergeant asked.

"Why, yes," she said "you do deal with public health matters don't you?"

I thought the sergeant was going to explode, his whole demeanour darkened and his fists clenched. This was the year that our Force topped one hundred thousand crimes for the first time and we were called to discuss flies! Then he calmed,

"I think we can help you madam."

"You can?"

"Yes. What you need," he started in his broad Yorkshire accent, "is a big bucket of shit."

I could have fallen off my chair and the woman looked horrified.

"Yes, madam. Horse shit would be best, and fresh. Put it under the kitchen window and leave a window open. There's nowt in here for flies and they love shit. Once they're out they won't come back in here. Have you finished your lemonade?"

As we walked to the car the woman was standing on her door stop as if she had been paralysed.

"Another satisfied customer," said the sergeant. "Put down in your notebook, 'Advice Given' ".

I never went back to see if the advice worked but I guess you could put it down as practical police work.

If that visit was one of the lighter moments, I was about to experience a darker one. You may remember the police officer I found in a hedge at my rugby club. He was now a detective inspector in a specialist unit and he was about to re-enter my life. I never saw him coming.

One day I was working away at a court file when I was asked to go and see a landlord who had just had his weekend takings stolen from his car. The complainant was waiting in his car about two miles from the station and I arrived there within quarter of an hour of his first ringing the Police.

Basically, his story was that he ran a fairly busy pub in the town and it was his practice to keep his Friday, Saturday and Sunday takings on the premises until Monday when he went to the bank and deposited it in his business account. On this occasion he had left his pub at about 10. am and put the takings in a brown envelope in the glove compartment of his car. He then set off to the bank but stopped at a newsagents close to where he was now parked. He locked the car and the glove compartment but when he came back to the car his takings were gone.

This might have seemed a fairly straightforward case where someone had studied his routine and waited for the right moment. However, the complainant claimed that the car was locked when he got back to it and the glove compartment was also secure. This would be unusual with either an opportunist theft or a planned one, unless someone had a duplicate set of keys for the car. I asked if anyone did have any keys or if his had gone missing.

At this stage the landlord became a little evasive; he firstly stated that no one would ever be able to get hold of his keys but eventually stated that his wife may have a set. I took a statement from him and said that I would be in touch. Later the same day I went to the pub to see the wife. A member of staff told me that she no longer lived with her husband but I was provided with her new address.

The wife was a pleasant woman. She laughed when I outlined the events that had been recounted to me. She was separated from her husband. She had never driven his car and had never seen or touched the car keys. Her husband owed her maintenance money but she said she did not expect to see it as the pub was struggling.

For a couple of days, I thought about this case while I also got on with other work. The original story did not ring true. The landlord had told me that he had over a thousand pounds in the glove compartment, roughly the amount that the wife said she was owed, but in those days, taking that amount of money would have been good trade for a struggling pub. Then there was the question as to why a thief who only had minutes to complete his/her crime would spend valuable seconds locking the car and glove compartment.

I decided to ask the landlord for proof of the amounts of his previous deposits and reluctantly he agreed that he would do so. I then had a visit from my friend from the hedge. He strolled into the CID office as if he owned it, told a constable to make him a cup of tea and then asked who was dealing with the theft of the takings. He came over and sat on the edge of my desk.

"I know you, don't I?" He asked.

"I don't think so." I replied in the hope of sticking to the present.

"I understand you are causing problems for a friend of mine."

"I don't think so. I'm just trying to find out the facts. So far it looks like it could be a false report."

"You must be new to this," he said. "My mates' wife is trying to take him to the cleaners and she has had his takings away. You should bring her in. Frighten her a bit and then whether she coughs or not he can make a claim."

"I don't see it like that, I'm waiting to see what his usual takings are…."

"You've no right to do that," he snapped. "Who do you think you are?"

I said nothing, he didn't seem to be listening.

"Do as I say if you want to stop in CID. We all drink in his pub and we should look after our own!"

I did not want to antagonize him too much but just as I had to respect his rank, I could not stop myself starting to feel aggressive towards him.

"I'll have a word with my boss, sir"

"You'll do what I'm telling you, now!"

"My boss is on duty this afternoon and I've told you what I'll do."

For just a moment I really thought he was going to hit me but there were witnesses in the office and he held back.

"Your fucking career is over." He said and stormed out of the office.

Eventually the landlord decided to change his story. He had probably not put the money in the glove compartment. He thought he might have taken it with him to the shop and dropped it. Also, surprise, surprise the amount he reported was drastically wrong he had made an error in the adding up. In the end my inspector 'No Crimed' the report, that is he accepted that the facts did not evidence that a crime had been committed and we were really dealing with a case of lost property! I thought the landlord should have been prosecuted but it would have been difficult to prove an offence and I was relatively happy that my old adversary had been put in his place. I was to have one more run in with him but that was not in the CID and it was many years later on a rugby trip.

One of the strangest things ever to happen to me came in my last days in the CID. It was a Sunday afternoon and it was snowing, large fluffy flakes that were drifting down and settling. I was seated in the control room with no reason to be there other than that it was warm and I was waiting to go home. An officer who lived well out of the town rang in to say that his car would not start and there was no bus service. He expected to be told to work from home but the control room sergeant was having none of it. I was asked to go and get him.

As I drove out of the built-up area the snow seemed to get thicker. Trees stood like black skeletons in the fading light and there were very few cars on the road. I drove up a steep, narrow hill and prepared to turn right onto a backroad that would soon be impassable. As I positioned my car for the turning a large, square, brick building loomed in the darkness directly ahead of me. This building was the ground level of a tall radio mast that towered overhead and provided a facility for all the Emergency Services operating in the area.

I would probably have hardly given it a look, but as I turned, I noticed a vehicle parked close up to the side of the building and thought I saw a light inside. In all my time working this area I had never seen anyone at the mast. I stopped and walked to the parked car. Its engine was warm in spite of the freezing weather and then I saw light inside the building again. It was obviously a torch and this did not seem right. I tried to radio my control room but in spite of my proximity to the mast they were not receiving.

I entered through the partially opened door and could hear someone moving inside the building. Then everything went quiet and the only thing I could hear was my own breathing. Suddenly a figure lurched towards me and I was pushed aside. The shadowy figure swept out from the building into the darkening, snowy world outside. I followed and saw footprints leading away from the road and towards a copse of trees.

There were no houses for miles in any direction and we were moving away from the road that passed the radio mast. I tried my radio again but with no more success than the first time. I then continued to follow the footprints that were clearly marked in the thickening snow.

As I chased the fleeing figure into the gloom, I heard him shout out and momentarily disappear from my view. He had tried to jump a barbed wire fence, caught it with his foot and fallen heavily. I arrived as he got to his feet and ran straight into him. We both went down and began to struggle. I recall, even now, that he was incredibly strong and I was beginning to wonder what I had got myself into. I shouted out that I was a police officer but he continued to struggle and then suddenly he spoke, "this is an exercise. I surrender".

He stopped struggling and allowed me to help him up, nor did he resist when I continued to hold his arm on the way back to the cars and the mast building. I tried the radio and found it still not working but I pretended to be talking to control and said that I was bringing a prisoner in.

As I drove back towards the station and the car heater started to make an impact my feet felt wet and I started to shiver. At the station I led my prisoner, a man of about my age with sandy hair, into the custody office. He refused to say anything to the sergeant or myself and in the end, he was searched and placed in a cell.

The man had no possessions other than a pack of cigarettes and it was later found that there was nothing in the car he had left at the radio mast. The car itself was blocked on the Police National Computer. I was sent home and told that I could do the interview when I came back in the morning.

When I did get back to work the prisoner was gone. I was asked what I had put in my notebook, which negligently, was nothing. The custody sergeant asked me if I had heard of the Official Secrets Act but he spoke in a manner which suggested he was joking. Finally, I was told not to talk about the incident as I had become involved in an exercise that was nothing to do with the Police.

To this day I do not know what was happening on the night I caught the 'mystery man'. Years later I heard a story told by an officer in a neighbouring Force. He claimed that the Special Boat Service had landed in rubber craft near an oil terminal in his area. They had evaded capture and placed dummy explosive devices at key points. The operation was to test security at key sites. I suppose I blundered into a similar exercise but no one ever told me or gave me any praise for detaining a 'saboteur'.

My time in the CID was coming to an end. I would not be going back to uniform patrol, the time had come for me to take my place on the Accelerated Promotion Scheme for which I had qualified many months earlier. The course, known then as the Special Course, ran for twelve months and marked the beginnings of an incredible and not always smooth journey through the ranks of the modern Police Service.

CHAPTER FOURTEEN

THE IVORY TOWER

Bramshill House was built in the Jacobean period by Lord Zouche and I am sure he would have been pleased with his creation. Situated in Hampshire, not far from the village of Hartley Wintney, the house can be approached, by road, from two directions. The main driveway stretches for almost a mile in a perfectly straight line. After passing through a small, arched gateway the drive drops fairly steeply to a white stone bridge, then rises towards the red brick house. On the left is an ornamental lake and on the right a deer park with a herd of white deer.

The house is a tall, imposing structure built out of small red bricks. It took some time for me to fully appreciate the magnitude and beauty of the building. I was a northern boy and our stately homes are usually built of sandstone or millstone, only the terraced houses of workers were routinely built of brick!

In 1959 Lord Brockett sold the house to the Home Office and it went on to fulfil numerous police related functions. For most police officers of rank, Bramshill was synonymous with the function of Staff College. I had tried to find out more about the place but in the days before the internet the only people I could have asked were senior police officers and as a constable I had had little contact with them.

In consequence, as I travelled down the M1 I had only a vague idea of how to get to Bramshill and no idea what I would find when I arrived. I did have great expectations and that in turn had led to a feeling of nervous anxiety. Not for one minute did I think that the others who were travelling to the College would be experiencing the same feeling.

The journey was over two hundred and fifty miles long and took me over five hours, much of the route was not on motorways. As I became established at the college, I sought out quicker and shorter routes. It became an obsession to try and complete the journey more quickly. Those attending the Special Course came from a number of Forces. There were three from Ireland and two or three from the extreme North East of England but the Force with the greatest representation was, unsurprisingly, the Met (The Metropolitan Police Force). They had eight officers out of the thirty course members and they had the big advantage that they could be home in little over an hour.

This may seem a strange thing to comment on but I regard it as particularly significant. The Met officers could go home on an evening and each weekend, they had many hours more at home than I did. The course lasted a year and although we were not at Bramshill the whole time I reckon they had the equivalent of eight working weeks more at home than I did. That is around three hundred and twenty hours when I was travelling; they could be studying, revising, drinking, attending concerts or sleeping! That was a big advantage by anyone's standards, as was the extra money they had by not spending huge amounts on petrol. For two weeks we attended an agricultural college in Lincolnshire where the Met officers had to travel north. One of them left the course immediately on returning to Bramshill and all of them spent time grumbling about being homesick!

All I will say is that it took me time to settle in at Bramshill and even then, when I came to love the place, I was less than enthusiastic about the course. We were divided into three groups each with a Chief Inspector to provide day to day support and some training inputs. There were also a number of academic staff led by Doctor John Watt.

The academics were a mixed bunch. The Head of Academic Studies was a brilliant man, short in stature he flitted around the college in an academic gown like a small bat. After he passed retirement age he remained at the college on some sort of grace and favour basis. He was always good company and helpful which could not be said of some of his colleagues. The overall quality of academic lecturing was, to say the least, average. Then again, the academic input was being provided to individuals with very different needs. The course had a student with a PHD., several graduates and also some with no previous academic background.

If the academics had an excuse for falling short, the Police input just did not seem to be professional in any way. Great emphasis was placed on physical fitness and yet we had no qualified instructor for any sporting activity. In consequence one of the Chief Inspectors had decided that he would double as a Physical Training Instructor. This individual, who would have been in his mid-forties at the time, did not look like he had ever had any involvement in sport. He had a distinct paunch, a flabby face and a thick, black walrus moustache. His track suit looked like it might have been issued thirty years previously and his canvas casuals completed a sorry picture.

Our first gym session took place in the college sports hall, a state-of-the-art facility with a full-sized football pitch/badminton court, weights room, squash courts and saunas. My fellow students included divers, a water polo champion, several rugby players, two marathon runners and various other good standard sports people. The chief inspector stood in front of us and tried to lead a warm up. "Touch your toes". He shouted and tried to touch his own. Failing dramatically to do that he shouted, "High Knees" and, holding the palms of his hands about three inches in front of his knees he tried to lift the latter to touch the former. The second failure did not deter him trying and failing to achieve several other warm up exercises.

The most exercise any of us got was stifling the laughs which his antics provoked. Then to make matters worse he lectured us on the need to get fitter if we wanted to complete the course.

In the confines of the college the failure of the staff to deliver professional physical training was mildly embarrassing but it did not stop there. The same mentality that led a flabby, middle-aged man to think he could do the training also led him to believe his pupils were capable of performing miracles. We were told that a sports evening had been arranged with a local semi-professional football team and that this would involve a football match and a bowling competition.

It seemed a good opportunity to get away from the college for a few hours. However, it was obvious from the beginning that the football would be a problem as only three or four of us had played football with any regularity. We only had nine pairs of boots between eleven players and five substitutes, the writing was well and truly on the wall.

As we drove into the ground, we saw that the match was advertised on hoardings outside the pitch. The clubs' turnstiles were open and people were actually paying to watch. We had no idea what had been said to the officials at the club but I am sure they did not expect the shambles that took place on their pitch. The score against us was in double figures before the second half really got started and the referee stopped the game at least quarter of an hour before he should have done.

In the changing room 'Mr High Knees' lectured us on the need to get fitter. I am amazed no one threw him out. The game of bowls or skittles that took place afterwards was not much better but it was at least warm in the bar and the beer was fairly cheap.

If Bramshill House was impressive and the sports facilities first class then it has to be said that our accommodation was of a similar standard to the physical training instructor. We were housed in a block of buildings known as the 'Quadrangle'. The reality was that a central square of lawn was surrounded on all four sides by residential blocks. Each block was connected to the next and had three storeys of single bedded study rooms.

On most days the accommodation was acceptable but the showers often ran cold early in the morning and the walls were wafer thin. In winter the central heating managed to collapse on an almost weekly basis. I remember one particular cold spell when there was snow on the ground. There was no heat at all in the classrooms and we were sent back to our bed/study rooms where we soon found that the central heating had given up altogether. We were issued with an extra blanket and from some of the rooms we could see steam rising through the snow where the hot water pipes had burst.

The food was both fairly good and a significant problem. The catering manageress, Mrs Dunlop, did a wonderful job with the budget that she was given. We could have three cooked meals a day, with coffee and biscuits mid-morning and tea and cakes mid-afternoon. There is something compulsive about eating free food, or there is for me, and eating became a habit that marked the passing of sections of the day. A typical day could be a full fried English breakfast, steak pie and chips with a warm pudding at lunchtime and beef wellington and cooked pudding in the evening. To all this a dietician would point out the copious quantities of beer and lager that were consumed when we were not eating!

On an evening, we had three bars to choose between in the grounds of the college. The most prestigious was in Bramshill House itself. The room was large with smaller sitting rooms leading off it. The wood panelled walls were decorated with plaques from Police Forces in all parts of the globe. To drink in the 'Mansion Bar' we had to wear a tie and this was not popular amongst many. However, this was the best location to meet individuals from courses other than your own. For me the Overseas Command Course had the most interesting and varied individuals.

One student that I got on with really well was a senior officer from a West Indian Force. Leonard was a large, muscular man with balding curly hair and his favourite occupation was watching television in the Mansion. One evening he was summoned to take a phone call at reception. He returned about ten minutes later with a big, broad grin spread across his face. He flopped back into his viewing chair and I asked if everything was alright.

"Oh Man! They was ringing me about this fella I arrested for shouting in the street. They wanted to know if he should be charged or bailed. Oh Man!"

At that time Leonard had been in England for nearly three weeks and the prisoner had been waiting for a decision as to what was to happen to him. Hopefully the Overseas Command Course focused on the concept of bail and human rights!

Throughout the 1980's there was always a large contingent of officers from the Royal Hong Kong Police Force. These individuals were, in my experience, always of Chinese origin though all of them had Christian names. Thus, I recall Charles Cheung, Clarence To and David Jang amongst others. They were always immaculately dressed, quite formal and almost invariably spoke excellent English with a Home Counties accent.

During the time I attended the Special Course the Police and Criminal Evidence Act of 1984 was in the early stages of becoming legislation. The Act was designed to create a code that would guide Police procedures and ensure that the public and prisoners were treat in a fair and equitable manner. It is true to say that there was considerable reaction and resistance to the introduction of the legislation. Rank and file police officers have a tendency to grumble and get on with things. More senior officers, in those days, were more vociferous and obstructive in their opposition to change.

The college ran a series of lectures on the 1984 Act and these were attended by officers from all the courses that were in progress at the time. I recall that one lecture was presented by a well-known and prominent academic. The audience was far less academic, certainly not impartial and after some twenty minutes a number of them became quite hostile.

The lecturer did his best to continue with his set talk but after a time it was clear that he was rattled and his temper was on the edge of snapping. He tried the risky tactic of asking those who were goading him questions about specific sections of the proposed legislation. For a time, this new approach worked and it was clear that some high ranking officers had little idea what was actually proposed. The lecturer should have quit while he was ahead. That he did not resulted in a near riot of laughter.

He picked out one of the Hong Kong officers and asked his name, which was Charles Cheung.

"Mr Cheung," began the academic, 'I am not certain what you know about the proposed legislation or how quickly it will be applied in your jurisdiction. What are your views on the Police and Criminal Evidence Bill?"

Now Charlie spoke Oxbridge English and was a very clever individual. He paused for a minute and then began to talk in a heavily accented Chinese/English.

"Yeh! Where in this Place Act it talking bout reccrodes?'

The lecturer clearly could not understand what was being said.

"I'm sorry Mr Cheung, could you repeat that?"

"Yeah. Where it talking bout reccrodes"

Still the lecturer was at a loss. He asked if anyone could interpret and the audience sat silently waiting for what happened next.

" You know. Flukking recrodes, blarreries for criminals."

At this point I became fully aware of what Charlie was talking about and realized that the whole thing was an act. I was clearly not alone as a Met Detective Superintendent spoke next,

"Mr Cheung is asking if the proposed legislation gives instructions regarding the use of electrodes and batteries in securing confessions."

The lecturer went silent, he was lost, the entire audience had understood what they had witnessed and were laughing and applauding uproariously. He collected his papers and slides and walked out of the lecture theatre. The laughter continued unabated.

"Flukking iriot!" Said Charlie and the room erupted again.

In the following days all sorts of memorandums and reports flew about the college advising staff to attend lectures with their students and ensure visitors were treated with respect. For me the event had been a learning experience. It was obvious that senior officers were often ill informed and unprepared when out of their own environment. The PACE Act was coming, no one could stop it and the arguments against it were as baseless as Charleys' question.

I remember another lecture that became quite controversial for different reasons. We were addressed by a Chief Officer from Lancashire, Joe Mouncey. He had been a senior detective during the Moors Murder investigation. I was fascinated to hear his take on Hindley and Brady but after all this time what I remember most is his calling the members of the Special Course a "set of Fucking Clones." I genuinely believe that recent years have seen many Chief Police officers become exactly that. I did not think he was right about us but then maybe he was more perceptive than me and saw what was coming!

I doubt he would have regarded us as clones if he had attended the two weeks that our course spent being tested in Wales. The trip was supposed to be a real challenge that would sort out the leaders from the hangers on. In my opinion the only people who were exposed were the organisers and supervisors who came with us.

We had to make our own way to a field in Wales where we were told to expect basic camping facilities. I decided that I would drive my car to the site and quickly attracted two passengers. I threw a small ruck sack in the boot of the car and set off in plenty of time. I picked up my first companion in Doncaster and he had slightly more with him in the way of clothes and 'extras', but the second pick up caused me to gasp in disbelief. My second passenger had a suitcase, a ruck sack a number of carrier bags and a tent with assorted camping gear. It was only just possible to get all of us and the luggage into the car and the handling of the vehicle for the rest of the journey was less than desirable.

At the camp site we found a field with toilets and two rows of matched tents. There was a stream running nearby and a shower block a short distance away. There was even a pleasant looking pub within walking distance. As we unpacked, our instructors were clucking around like mother hens. Mr High Knees was present looking like he couldn't wait to get started. The head of the course, a Chief Superintendent, looked like a latter-day Baden-Powell in khaki shorts, knee length woollen socks and a khaki shirt. The only thing he lacked for the full Boy Scout ensemble was a toggle!

During the days we spent in Wales we negotiated an Army Assault Course and I remember one of the girls, who went on to become a Chief Constable, slipping off a rope and ending in a flooded ditch with frogs hopping on and off her. For most though the test was an experience to be remembered but not a great challenge. We had another test where we were to use the basics of map reading to get back to the camp site. The instructors set out early to put one or two markers on the twenty-mile course. Unfortunately, they were so slow that we had caught sight of them within an hour and we followed them at a distance without once needing to look at the map!

After a couple of evenings, we were sat round a fire when I saw one of my passengers from the trip to Wales engaged in deep discussion with the course leader. One or two of us edged nearer to hear what was happening. It went something like,

"Sir. I've got my tent with me and as I'm one of the few coping with the course I thought I could help out a bit. I could go up the hill and bring weather forecasts down in the morning."

To our amazement this was agreed and off he went with his own tent up a high hill where there was no toilet or washing facilities. The next morning, he came back to say the day was set to be fair and the day later, as we struggled into waterproofs, he announced that it was going to rain. After several days of this he was told to come back down and re-join the group which he did, setting himself up as an amateur camp chiropodist. Several individuals ended up with septic blisters after his ministrations.

The same individual also distinguished himself by being shown to be something of a fraud. One evening as we sat round the fire drinking beer and getting louder and louder, he was slurring his words with the best of us. Then when he went to the toilet a future high ranking Met officer decided to drink his beer. The problem was that the beer can did not have beer in it. Our weather forecasting, chiropodist colleague was drinking water out of a beer can and pretending to be drunk. This was priceless and resulted in a serious sense of humour loss when we told him we knew.

There is more to say about this individual but I do not want to get out of sequence. The visit continued without becoming too onerous. We did a 'river crossing' which could have been quite dangerous, especially as it was organized by High Knees. However, all I remember of that day is catching one of the instructors peeking at the girl course members as they dried off behind a car.

Then one night, after we had all been to the pub, we were woken at two in the morning and told that a girl had gone missing in a quarry about two miles away. This, we were told, was a real incident and we were given temporary ranks to deal with it. The course member put in command of the incident immediately asked for radio contact with the local Force so he could ask for lights and back up. He was told he could not have it and this led to an outcry.

Under pressure the instructors admitted it was not a real incident and we had to manage with our existing staff and resources. Someone asked if it was a real quarry and the whole thing started to plunge into chaos. It was a disused slate quarry which the map showed had numerous tunnels and pits. When I was put in charge of a search I refused to go into the quarry until day light and was told that I must act immediately. To me the whole situation was unsafe. There was no one to save, it was pitch black, we had three torches and no ropes. I refused and was replaced by another individual.

If the visit to Wales was a pleasant distraction the same could not be said of the assessments that took place when we returned to the college. Our behaviour was minutely dissected and reports were written that were serious in nature and often quite derogatory in content. I, along with many others, could not believe that a mismanaged farce could be the basis of what was, in many cases, character assassination.

As we settled back into college routine some individuals were not allowed to forget their conduct in Wales. Practical jokes had become a daily event and now seemed to take on a whole new dimension. One of the ringleaders was nicknamed 'Damien' and, later in his career, he became the Commissioner of the Metropolitan Police

Damien had taken exception to my travelling companion referring to himself as the only person 'coping with that trip'. That same individual had brought an inflatable arm chair to the college from his home in Yorkshire. The chair, when inflated, was a huge, purple monstrosity that took up all the spare floor space in his bed/study room. Damien waited until everyone was on the way to a lecture then climbed up a drainpipe and into the room holding the chair. He deflated it and departed with the purple plastic seat up his jumper.

When the chairs' owner found that it was missing, he was apoplectic. He stormed from room to room accusing people of stealing his chair and pointing out that the events constituted burglary. He was laughed at everywhere he went and his temper became more and more tested.

Two days later we had been on a coach trip to see a computerized crime system being developed by a Force near the college. We were dropped off in the main car park and had to climb two long sets of steps that ran up a wooded slope. The Beech and Birch trees over hung the steps and it was always quite a gloomy approach to our accommodation. As we climbed the steps, I was among the many students to notice the inflated purple chair dangling on a rope from the branch of a beech tree. It was central to the steps and about a meter above head height. It could not be missed, though its' owner pretended to do so. Several days later he recovered the chair floating on one of the lakes in the grounds.

If he thought that the practical jokers would now shift their attention to others then he was very wrong. A number of weeks later he received a letter on the Commandants' note paper telling him that a Superintendent on another course was planning to take some teenagers camping. He was seeking advice from experienced people and the Commandant had recommended that they get together. Later the same day my companion got another note, purporting to be from the Superintendent, and asking if they could meet for a chat in the Mansion Bar that evening.

When he arrived for his meeting, he should have registered that, unusually, our entire course was already in the bar. Shortly the barman received a phone call telling him that the Superintendent had left the Mansion Bar and was in the pub just down the road. This information was duly passed on and our fellow course member set off into the foggy evening to find the person wanting his advice.

From the phone box in the side entry to Bramshill House, Damien then rang the pub and asked them to tell a gentleman, who would be looking for Superintendent X, that that individual had moved on to another pub. He repeated the exercise several times as our colleague drove from pub to pub trying to find the imaginary person who wanted his advice.

Nearly three hours later Damien caused his victim to return to the college. He walked into the bar looking cold and fed up.

As he asked the barman if the Superintendent had returned, he was handed a carrier bag. He took a large object from the bag and found it to be a piece of polished slate. It was inscribed with the words "Coping Stone." Only then did he realize he had been the victim of a practical joke and he stormed out into the night.

I could write a whole book about the pranks, jokes and supposed 'jolly japes' that helped us through the sometimes mundane and boring days. They came to an abrupt end, however, with one of the most elaborate of them all backfiring on its' organizer.

With almost everyone at the college being miles from home it would have been surprising if there had not been affairs and extra marital liaisons. What amazed me was that there seemed to be so few of them! Perhaps the reason lay in the fact that we were such a close-knit group and affairs disrupted routine. I do not know the real reason but I do know that Damien and others, who made up a small drinking club, were irritated that one of their members had the audacity to be sleeping with a female at the college. On an evening this reprobate would make his way to his girlfriends' room and then return to his own bed just before lectures started the following morning.

This went on for some time until one morning the 'lover' was returning from his night out. It was a sunny morning and the birds were singing as he walked alongside the lake in the centre of the college grounds. He was at peace with the world and then he paused, started to walk again and finally stopped completely. On an island in the middle of the lake he could make out items of police uniform hung on trees and in bushes. Then he saw a wardrobe, a desk, a chair and various other items that belonged in a bed/study room and not on a muddy, tree covered island.

Walking on he was probably amused that someone had played a prank on an unsuspecting colleague. Only on arriving at his own empty room did he realize what had happened. He had a lot to do, he would certainly miss breakfast.

As we collected in a lecture hall after having eaten the usual full English breakfast, we noted that our colleague was missing. Most of us did not know what had happened. Unusually, all three instructors were present and shortly afterwards the Chief Superintendent arrived looking very serious. He stood at the front of the room and addressed us in what I am sure he believed was a 'Churchillian' manner. Basically, the story was that our colleague had found his belongings on the island and secured a boat in order to bring them back to dry land. While doing so he had been seen by the duty security officer. There had been an altercation that got out of hand and the result was that the practical jokes victim had been returned to his Force. This would mean that his career was in tatters. There was total silence until coffee break when everyone wanted to talk about what had happened.

As we chatted away, I did not notice that Damien was missing. He had slipped away as soon as the lecture finished and as we expressed our opinions, he was making his way to the Commandants office to confess. He marched in and started to explain that he was responsible for our colleague's departure. Only gradually did he realize that no one in the Commandants' office knew anything about what he was telling them. Damien was the victim of a secondary practical joke. All our instructors had conspired with the 'victim' to give Damien a lesson. They did not realize that the practical joke king would be willing to make the ultimate sacrifice.

The result was that no one left the course but all the instructors were advised about their future conduct. Damien also received a really good dressing down which I suspect would have been worse if anyone had known about his stealing the Commandants' note paper for the earlier escapade.

Practical jokes almost ceased but Damien had one last trick up his sleeve. A sergeant from his own Force was pursuing a female Police Cadet who was one of a number at the college to provide support for the instructors. After a lengthy courtship the sergeant was seen entering the cadets' residential block. Two hours later he was still there. Damien elicited the help of a number of our course. We put boot polish on our faces, wore the nearest things we had to camouflage gear and all donned balaclavas then set off on the mission. We climbed into an open window on the upper floor of the girls block and asked a terrified cadet where our colleague was. After a fair degree of banging a door was opened and we had found the bedroom of the female who was the object of our colleagues' desires. She was wearing a night dress but there was no sign of him. Then we heard a noise and realized that someone was hiding inside the wardrobe. Damien rocked the wardrobe onto its side and we picked it up and set off out of the room. The wardrobe was not big but with a male police officer in it handling became a problem. As we got to the top of the stairs leading out of the building we were halted.

A female Chief Inspector stood at the bottom of the flight of stairs. I only knew she was a Chief Inspector because I recognized her. On this occasion she was wearing a pink nightdress and her hair was in curlers. There was nothing wrong with her vocal cords and she screamed at us like a Drill Sergeant Major on parade. The wardrobe slipped from our grasp, bumped on the floor and then slid down the stairs. It gathered speed as it approached the bottom and splintered into numerous pieces when it got there. Among the wooden chunks of what had been a fine piece of furniture lay a police sergeant naked but for his underpants. Years later he was to become the Deputy Chief Constable of a large northern Force but you would not have foreseen that as he tried to scramble to his feet and get out of the building.

We were all disciplined and advised about our duty, to the families of the young cadets, to ensure that they were not taken advantage of. Then we got on with the course.

I have already mentioned the trip to rural Lincolnshire that we undertook and no account of the Special Course would be complete without at least some reference to what took place there. Like much of our course, the idea behind going to Lincolnshire was sound; it was in converting the theory to reality that usually caused a problem.

The idea was that we would be based in an Agricultural College while the usual students were on holiday. We would use the local village and surrounding area as a sort of set for various practical exercises. Things were supposed to seem real because there were real people and real places all around us with just a few role players added for good measure.

It must have been quite unnerving for the local residents as they became the most over policed area in England and Wales. Those who noticed this presence must also have wondered why all the police were now sergeants. If the residents had been alert, they would have also seen two Firearms incidents unfold, a hostage situation, a bomb at the local church and a major traffic accident.

For those of us taking part in the exercises the most challenging thing was riding the bicycles that we were provided with. Most of them were too small for any of the male members of the course and more than one of them had seriously defective brakes. Anyone who has actually been to Lincolnshire will know that there are some serious hills in various parts of the county and one of those led from the college to the village. The ride to the incidents was a white-knuckle affair and the trip back was a long, tiring trudge.

One of our course members, I will call him Peter, had been dealing with a disturbance at the pub. He had successfully dealt with the staged events that were laid on for him and he was making his way back to the college. As he did so he saw a car slowly mount a kerb and almost carefully crash into the wall of a garden. Peter thought that this was an exercise and could not believe that he was supposed to tackle two practical's one after another. He waited for another course member to arrive and when no one did he walked over to the car. The driver was sat in his car drinking from a bottle. Peter told the driver that he would arrest him and take him to the station, expecting the driver, as an actor to confirm that that was the correct course of action. "Thank you." Said the driver. "Can you help me get the car back on the road?"

Peter helped the man push the car off the wall and onto the main road. He thought the instructor was behaving a bit strangely but could not think of anything else he could do as part of the scenario. So, placing his bike in the pub car park for later collection, Peter asked the man for a lift to the college. This was provided without incident and it was only later that everyone found out that the man had been a real drunken driver and the wall he hit was quite badly damaged. Further, the householder who reported the damage had also seen the offending car drive off with a policeman in it. I was glad I did not have to explain how this had happened to the real local police!

If a real incident was badly botched then some of the 'pretend' ones were not handled much better. A future Chief Constable was taken hostage by a gunman and bundled into a barn down a narrow lane. The barn was surrounded and another future Chief Constable was called upon to play the role of a negotiator. The 'gunman' demanded that the negotiator approach the barn so he could hear him. This was approved by the course member in overall command. The gunman then said he suspected the negotiator was 'wired' and asked that he be told to take his shirt off. The 'commander' ordered the negotiator to comply. Standing shirtless within ten meters of a barn occupied by a gunman the negotiator was literally exposed to further danger when the gunman ordered him to take his trousers off to ensure he did not have a weapon. Again the 'commander' supported the request and the future Chief was left standing in his underpants on a cold autumn day while observers tried to conceal their giggles.

All in all, I quite enjoyed the trip to Lincolnshire, it might have had the usual element of Keystone Cops but at least it seemed designed to achieve something. This view was not shared by the Met officers who had a four-hour drive home and seemed permanently on the point of open revolt. For me, the two-hour journey was one third of the usual trek and then I was off to Bradford for a week "work experience". The idea was that each of us chose a Force very different from their own and made a study of an area of policing they had not previously experienced.

I chose to look at policing a racially diverse area. I had only seen two black faces in all my time working the streets of my Force. Bradford was certainly very different in having a large Asian population. The only problem was that someone in Bradford decided I would be less trouble if I worked nights and I saw very little of the Asian community. I did spend several nights with Brian Noble who was a well-known rugby league player as well as a police sergeant. Brian went on to play for and coach Great Britain and is now a sports commentator on television as well as having been Director of Rugby for Toronto Wolfpack (Rugby Leagues then newest team)

When we returned to the college from our various visits the atmosphere began to change. We had to take the Police Inspectors' examinations as well as the college academic exams. The thought of having to study for the promotion exams in such a short period of time was quite perturbing. There was a massive amount of work. However, as usual things did not turn out as I thought. One by one the instructors let slip the subjects that we would be examined on and while we began by believing we were being lulled into a false sense of security, it became clear we were not. No one got less than eighty per cent in the police exams. Considering that we only had two weeks to prepare we must have had the intellects of super humans.

No one complained about the ease of passing; though I bet those who had to take the exams subject to the usual rules would have done. Further, the fact that ten marks separated the top of the course from the bottom rendered the assessment process a farce. The tiny difference in marks related more to the quality of the instructors 'slips' than to the student's ability.

In the years after I completed my Special Course the duration was shortened and split into modules. It seemed a much better system but I cannot comment on the quality of what was delivered. I do not think many courses could have had a higher performance than ours had in producing the very top officers.

Socially the college was a wonderful experience. Nowadays with the amount of eating and drinking it would have to carry a health warning. Some of the ways we entertained ourselves would also fail the politically correct test. I remember three of us, all male and two with moustaches, 'blacking up', wearing dresses and high heels as a Three Degrees tribute act. However, we created a pretty fair rugby team that won most of its' Wednesday afternoon games. We were even allowed to go and play against army officers at Sandhurst, though we had to eat in a pavilion outside the army Staff College, because we were not 'real officers.

Leaving was as a shock to the system. We didn't want to go but we hadn't really wanted to be there. It was a means to an end and all but two of us had survived. To the officer who left after the Lincolnshire trip must be added another individual. He was caught plagiarizing/copying someone else's work for the final course assessment. He had to leave the course but over the years he probably did not lose much by this.

So, we packed our bags, loaded our cars and set off back to the 'real World'. For some it was to be a painful experience and I was one of those unfortunate ones.

CHAPTER FIFTEEN

CENTRAL HELL

Several weeks before I finally left Bramshill, I received a report informing me that I was posted to the city sub division where I had started my career as a constable. I was quietly pleased by this for a number of reasons. I knew people there and had always got along with everyone. As a new sergeant, I was pleased because the duties were more predictable than in a rural area. There would be shoplifters by the score, drunks, disorder, lost children and licensing offences. There were rarely any fatal collisions, no poaching, fewer murders and it was Sleepy Hollow after the pubs and clubs had closed.

On my first day back, I must admit to a slight buzz as I walked down the main corridor of the station. This was the first time I had worn my sergeants' stripes in a real police station and it felt good. I was amazed how quickly personnel had changed. On the relief to which I was posted I recognized none of the fifteen constables and only one of the other sergeants. However, everyone was very friendly and I quickly found a locker for my uniform.

There is no doubt that for a few hours I walked around with a mild feeling of euphoria. I should have gone home while it lasted but I hadn't yet got a home and I did have a meeting with the sub divisional commander. George Henry Stanley was by all accounts a strange man. Nobody liked him but no one was very forthcoming about the things that made him unpopular.

He kept me waiting in the corridor outside his office for the best part of an hour. Then, when I had been admitted to his office, he sat reading or looking at a report on his desk without ever once paying me any attention. Eventually he looked up and seemed genuinely surprised to see me there. Still, he said nothing and commenced tidying numerous separate piles of paper on his desk.

His hair was combed back from his forehead and it gave the appearance of being dyed. In every other way he was immaculate.

"Why are you special?" He asked, suddenly breaking the silence.

I had no idea what he wanted me to say. It was obvious that he was referring to my having been on the Special Course.

"I don't think I am special, Sir. I have just been lucky enough to have been on a course of that name."

He peered at me and then put on a pair of glasses that I had not seen previously.

"I wasn't good enough for that course and I want to know what is special about you?"

There we were. Five minutes in his office and it was clear we were not going to get on. It was also clear to me why that was going to be the case. I said nothing and waited.

"Well, I expect you to be special. I will be watching to make sure you are better than all the other sergeants and woe unto you if you fall short. For now, you can do me a paper on what makes a police officer special."

I never, in all my service heard anyone else required to perform a task like that. It did not seem fair but then I was to learn that, whatever else George Henry might be, he certainly was nor fair.

Then he quite simply told me to get out. Not welcome to the sub division, no cosmetic greeting, just a curt command to get out. So, I did as I was told.

The days ticked by and I gave George Henry his paper. Thirty years later I am still waiting to hear what he thought of it. I also did my best to get a feel for the capabilities and workloads of those constables who worked for me. Helping them was relatively easy because the majority were not very experienced and had not developed bad habits.

Not long after I arrived, we were told that the station was to be visited by one of Her Majesty's Inspectors of Constabulary. These individuals, usually known as HMI's, were in those days almost exclusively retired Chief Constables who visited Police Forces on behalf of the Home Office to ensure that things were being done properly. In later years the HMI's tended to identify best practice in dealing with an aspect of police work then assess everyone against the best practice benchmark. However, things were much more primitive in the early 1980's.

The HMI's checked officers' notebooks, assessed standards of cleanliness, smartness and generally focused on seeking out polite enthusiasm. When they left, they submitted reports and anything negative resulted in shoutings and screamings from the senior officers and everyone else running around putting things into a proper state.

I was relieved to note that the HMI was to arrive as I would be going off duty. We would not meet. On the day of the inspection, I ensured that all my constables had put their equipment away in their lockers and that our work books were bang up to date.

I ensured that all my own uniform was properly put away and the desks were clear. I then went home. I only know what happened next from what the people involved told me and it went like this. Dick Milne was coming on duty; he was wearing the same shirt he had had on the day before but changed it when he arrived at work so as to be ready for the inspection.

Running late he performed the shirt changing in the sergeant's office and as he was about to take the dirty shirt to his locker the HMI was walking down the corridor. He shoved the shirt in an open drawer, closed it and left the room. The HMI, a staff officer and George Henry entered the sergeant's office a few minutes later. The HMI saw a shirt sleeve hanging out of the drawer and joked that someone had been in a hurry. George Henry went apoplectic. The shirt was in a drawer I shared with another sergeant.

The following day I was summoned to the commanders' office and subjected to a verbal tirade about standards and lack of cleanliness. I tried to tell him that the shirt was not mine and that we had to share drawers but he was not interested. Once again, he told me to get out. By this time, I had temporarily moved into a police house and I recall getting home, slamming the door shut and sitting thinking of what I could do to George Henry.

I met him again only days later and once again he vented his wrath on me. The house I had been allocated was fine, though the garden was overgrown and the previous occupant, clearly a wine maker, had left scores of bottles. I had no curtains and was not in a hurry to buy any as my stay in the house was supposed to be short. When I next saw George Henry, it was because a resident from near my house had rung in to say it was untidy. I had been there six days.

Again, I tried to tell him what I had inherited but this time I had no chance. I should have reported flaws when I got the keys to the house and having witnessed my mother and fathers house being inspected, I should have known procedures. The thing that really got to me was the manner of his attack.

"You are doing this on purpose." He stated as if he was the victim of some attack on his person.

"Are you a queer?"

I could not believe what I was hearing. In our current age he would have been in real trouble but he knew and I knew that he was safe from censure.

"I can assure you I am not." I said, trying to sound indignant.

"Well, look at you. Thirty years old and not married. You need a wife. You can't wash your shirts; you can't keep your house clean and you are determined to upset me."

I didn't know what to say. There was no one to complain to, no recourse.

"Women are bloody useful for stuff like ironing." He said.

I left his office not far short of tears. It was so frustrating. Some of the individuals who had been at Bramshill with me had quickly become friends with their bosses, they went for a drink together and were given specific learning experiences. I got George Henry Stanley. I also got Geordie Mannion and my dealings with him would achieve the impossible, it made things even worse.

Constable Mannion was a large fleshy individual with a fresh complexion and rosy cheeks. He had a broad North East accent and I sometimes had to concentrate carefully to assure myself he was speaking English. When I arrived back from Bramshill he had just been allowed to commence independent patrol. I quickly came to wonder how anyone could have thought he was ready for that responsibility.

Not far from the city station there was a square, surrounded on all sides by buildings. The buildings all housed shops and the rear of those premises opened onto the square. A narrow lane led into the square and this provided access for delivery vehicles and customers who were collecting larger articles in their cars.

During my first set of night shifts, after returning to real policing, I was walking towards the square. It was a cool night but there were spots of rain in the wind and the pavements were already wet. As I passed the entrance to the square PC Mannion was walking out. We exchanged greetings and I asked him if anything had been happening on his beat.

"Way I, sergeant," he started and then, looking really enthusiastic, "I've just met a real nice man. He'd been closing the windows of a shop so the rain wouldn't get in"

This immediately rang alarm bells for me. What was the man doing in the square at this time in the morning? The shops had been closed for hours and it was still hours before they opened again. I asked PC Mannion to show me where the man had been.

"Why, he was there sergeant." He said pointing to a distant corner where several drainpipes descended from the roofs above.

"So, was he at the bottom of the drain pipes when you saw him? "I asked.

"Why, no. He was coming down from shutting the windows. I helped him, like."

I am sure most people reading this will find what was said unbelievable, I did at the time, but it is as near word for word as my interpretation of Geordie can get.

The drainpipes were at the back of a jeweller's shop and as we stood there the alarm began to ring. The man had been in the shop. PC Mannion had helped a burglar descend a drain pipe and not noticed a carrier bag of stolen items that the man had just acquired. At Bramshill we had been told that a uniform officer could randomly patrol the streets for years and never come across a burglary in progress. I was responsible for an officer who not only came across a burglar but helped him on his way.

To be fair to the officer we did catch the burglar and recovered most of what he had stolen. This success was, however, almost as miraculous as coming across the burglar in the first place. PC Mannion liked motorcycles and the burglar had one in the square, further the officer had a photographic memory and remembered the registration number. From this we traced the offender at an army camp in the north of England.

If this had been a one-off display of ineptitude it would probably have been quickly forgotten about. However, within days I was called to the officers' lodgings. There I found his landlady in a distraught state. As soon as I entered the house the lady took me to the kitchen, there she lifted a table cloth and underneath the table I saw a large cardboard box.

"Pull it out." She instructed me.

So, I bent and pulled the box from under the table, noting as I did so that there were several pairs of large Doctor Martin's boots and shoes in it. I was bemused.

"There's five pairs in there," she said. "I told him when he came to get his feet under the table and feel at home. Then the boots started arriving. Is he alright in the head?"

She then took me upstairs and into a clean, tidy and reasonable sized bedroom.

"Look under there," she said, indicating the bed.

Again, I stooped and lifted up the quilt covering the bed. There under the bed were numerous plates, each with what looked like cooked meals on them and covered with cling film.

"I cook for him every day and if I'm at work all he has to do is warm it up on the plate. I started to run out of plates and then I found them. There are twelve meals under his bed and some have been there for nearly two weeks. It's not fair." She was obviously close to tears.

We made our way down stairs and she told me about the "dirty magazines" that she kept finding in various locations. Her concern was not her lodger's moral welfare but what her visitors would think when they found porn in the bathroom or the pantry. I said that I would speak to PC Mannion and that I was sure things would improve.

The officer did not see what he was doing was wrong. He didn't like her cooking and was too shy to say. He was also adamant that he had been told to get his boots under the table not his feet and he was only doing what he was told. As regards the magazines well, "we all use Porn" was his response. Fortunately, he decided to look for alternative accommodation.

My next dealing with him was as I came out an interview room. He looked totally perplexed and I tried to help!

"Sergeant, I was just writing a ticket for a car on double yellows. Outside the front of the station, like. Then this 'teccy' came and got in and drove off. I don't know what to do with the ticket. With it being one of us like."

I thought this was relatively easy to sort out but I made the mistake of giving him options to try and start a thought process.

"Well, you could do one of three things," I said.

"You could write out the ticket and do a report saying exactly what has happened. Advantage, someone else will decide if the detective gets the ticket. Or you could complete the ticket and issue it to the detective when you see him or thirdly, you could write 'SPOILED" on the ticket and hope no one asks what happened. I guess you could also throw the ticket away. Now, what are you going to do?"

"Well, it's obvious sergeant, when you put it like that. Thank you."

Before I got chance to say anything else another officer interrupted, he needed my assistance with a prisoner we had been interviewing.

I thought no more about the parking ticket over the next two weeks. Then out of the blue I was told that George Henry wanted to see me. As usual he kept me waiting in the corridor, as usual he ignored me when I eventually gained admittance to his office. Then he looked up and peered at me over his gold rimmed glasses.

"I give up with you," he said. "You are not special, I have watched and seen no evidence that you are anything but ordinary. Now I wonder if you are even ordinary. How can you tell a P.C. to tear up a parking ticket? How?"

I was staggered. There was a long pause while I wondered whether it was worth saying anything.

"I have not told anyone to tear up a ticket. I told a P.C. he had a number of options and tried to make him take responsibility......"

"Don't give me that Mumbo Jumbo. You've got it in for that lad"

"That lad is absolutely useless. He should not be on independent patrol, he is...."

"Out, get out of my office. You are not fit to be a supervisor. The Lad wants help not some queer picking at him."

I walked out. Then I went to see my inspector. He told me that he thought George Henry was "Mad as a Hatter". He said that our superintendent had once lectured him about women having a permanent discharge just because he had separated from his wife. Having an ally calmed me down but it did not help. A week later I was called to see the Divisional Commander. Things were not good.

The visit to Divisional Headquarters was surreal. I sat in the Commanders' waiting room with two other officers waiting to be disciplined. One of them, another sergeant, had been drinking himself into oblivion for many weeks. His wife had left him and he lived in a house with almost no furniture. On one occasion he had to be sent home from work because he had maggots in his hair. On the occasion that caused him to be present this time he had also been very drunk. He had been drinking home brew for hours and then decided to borrow a bike from his neighbours' garden in order to get to work. The bike was a small pink one belonging to an eight-year-old girl. At a major junction on his journey his leg shot off the pedal and he fell onto the road with the bike laying on top of him.

The other officer had attacked his father-in-Law and all but wrecked a brand-new kitchen. As the large wall clock ticked away loudly, I could not help thinking that my presence was totally unjust. I had done nothing other than have the misfortune of having the wrong superintendent.

The drunken bike thief was given advice about his future conduct and advised to see his doctor. The attacker was moved to a different station and I was told that I would not be promoted to inspector at the end of my year as a sergeant. That promotion was guaranteed by my having completed the Special

Course so delaying it was a major event. The Home Office would have to be informed and I was told that the Chief Constable would have to tell me in person.

This was the lowest feeling I had ever experienced in my life. I wanted to cry out and tell everyone. I started drinking just to get drunk. Then I went to see the Chief and things started to slowly get better. I was still to be regarded as on the Accelerated Promotion Scheme; the only difference was that I had to serve an extra six months as a sergeant.

From the minute I went back to the station the atmosphere was different. Two Chief Inspectors asked to see me and both were helpful and friendly. I was given lots of little projects to manage which went well and then I was asked to become my reliefs Custody Sergeant. This was a responsible job that usually only went to experienced sergeants. Then George Henry was moved to another station and the sun came out again.

Several years later, still miraculously a serving Police Officer, Geordie Mannion was also working in the Custody Office. Half an hour after his shift had started the sergeant could not find him. An hour later he was still not present and the sergeant was trying to manage the needs of some fifteen prisoners. Eventually, the Matron who looked after female prisoners, came and asked the sergeant if she could have her office back. P.C.Mannion had brought a young female into work with him, they had gone in the Matron's Office and shut the door. Now moaning noises were to be heard in the corridor. The sergeant walked in expecting to see some sort of pornographic display. There on the floor lay the officer and his female companion. Both were wearing sunglasses in the darkened room and they had headphones on. The moaning was the cries of whales from a cassette recording. Both of them were fast asleep.

I will make no further comment about this constable other than to say he retired in 2011 having completed thirty years as a Police Officer......utterly amazing.

Being a Custody Sergeant was regarded as one of the most responsible jobs in the Force. The role was spelled out in the Police and Criminal Evidence Act and this basically made the postholder the most important person in relation to custody. You could refuse to accept a prisoner if you were not satisfied that there were grounds for arrest, you could release a prisoner if you did not feel that the investigation was proceeding promptly and efficiently. Further you recorded everything that happened to the prisoners, you were responsible for their welfare and you had to ensure they received everything they were entitled to.

The staff in the Custody Office that I worked in consisted of myself, a constable and a matron. We often had in excess of twenty prisoners but it was only at peak times that we had to call for assistance. Much of the time we had little to do but you could never relax because of the nature of the people you came into contact with. Further, that comment did not only apply to the prisoners. I often had as many problems with police officers as I did with those in the cells.

One prisoner, to me, always summed up the vagaries of human nature. Tommy Berry was a forger. He was a fully-fledged professional who could have made a good living as an artist or an engraver. He came into my Custody Office more than once but the second time he was remanded to police cells for the purpose of facilitating the investigation of alleged offences. It was claimed that he had forged numerous benefit books with intent to defraud the Department of Health and Social Security. I saw one of the books and it was a work of art.

While in our cells it became evident that he was used to being held in custody. He was quickly sweeping up, helping deliver meals to other prisoners, organizing a timetable for showers and other useful tasks. The cleaners who came in twice a day thought he was wonderful. He drew one of them a Penny Black stamp which looked just like the real thing and they in return made him cups of coffee and gave him sweets and chocolate. After the first day he started making a Gipsy caravan out of paper plates and other bits and pieces of rubbish that he collected. This caravan was a wonder to behold, officers came into the cell block just to see it as it progressed from a pile of litter to a really impressive scale model.

As the time for Tommy leaving approached the cleaners bought him a special meal from the police canteen which, in a moment of kindness, we allowed him to have. Tommy in turn promised to leave the cleaners his finished model caravan.

As he departed through the rear door of the Custody Office to be conveyed back to prison the cleaners waved him off. They then went to collect their model caravan. I filled in the Custody Sheet that recorded his time with us and placed it in the tray for filing. Suddenly the peace was shattered.

"The dirty Bastard." I heard one of the cleaners cry.

"The filthy pig." The other one added.

I entered the cell block and there on the concrete floor was Tommy's caravan and a pile of human excrement. The caravan had been finished to perfection and for good measure its' creator had seen fit to shit in it. The cleaner had picked it up and the mess had fallen through the bottom. What would possess anyone to behave like that? Tommy had been well treated and almost adored by the cleaners. Further, with his track record he must have known that it was only a matter of time before he would be back in our custody. Unbelievable in many ways but this sort of behaviour was regularly on display in our Custody Office.

Nor can I say that the failings of human nature only manifested themselves in the criminal visitors. There were numerous occasions where police officers behaved in sub human ways.

Detectives were not my favourite people when I was working in the Custody Office. They had a tendency to think that they could bend the rules and that securing a detection was the only consideration. Ethics often went out of the window and it was necessary to watch them like a hawk.

Interviews were supposed to be conducted in Interview Rooms. The prisoners had to be booked out and on their return the length of the interview was recorded. Sometimes we became so busy that interviewing officers had to wait in line to be dealt with and it was then that they often tried to take advantage. They would let themselves in through the side door and come out behind the position where my staff and I would be processing prisoners. They would then try and pick up a set of cell keys and surreptitiously disappear down the cell block.

On one occasion I was busy getting a batch of prisoners ready for court. We were handing bags of personal belongings over to the staff who would convey those prisoners to their hearings. This required care and attention because lots of things could go wrong. Suddenly, there was a bang from the direction of the cell block. I thought a door had been slammed shut but no one should have been there so I sent my warder to check.

Almost as soon as the warder had gone two detectives strolled into the Custody Office, having clearly come from the cell block. I asked them to wait for me to finish with the Court prisoners but in the confusion, they slipped off.

When my warder returned, he said that everything appeared to be in order and usually that would have been an end of things. However, for some reason I decided to go and double check. As I looked into one of the cells, I saw that its occupant was kneeling on the floor with tears rolling down his cheeks. I entered the cell and noticed two or three polystyrene cups on the window ledge. The cell had a strange smell to it but I could not immediately say what it was.

It transpired that the detectives had entered the cell nearly an hour earlier as we started processing the departing prisoners. They had started to ask the inmate to confess the offence for which he was in custody. At one stage he had asked to go to the toilet and they had made him urinate in the cups, even though each cell had a toilet. According to the prisoner they had then knelt him on the floor and produced a gun which they placed at the back of his head. He had not believed for a minute that police officers would shoot him, but his world had fallen apart when the gun went off. His ears hurt so much that he thought he had been shot.

This was serious by any standards. The detectives had not recorded anything on the prisoners Custody Record, so in theory they had never been there. I called the Discipline and Complaints Department and then got on with the chores of the day. I was interviewed by a Chief Superintendent who told me at length that I had not really witnessed anything and that I was providing him with hearsay (something I had been told by others). My warder had seen and heard nothing so it was the prisoners' word against that of the detectives. In the end they were given advice about not entering the Custody Office and cell block without permission. That was it.

I was certain, in retrospect, that what I had noticed in the cell block was the smell of gunpowder but I could not prove this. The prisoner eventually asked me to stop trying to find evidence because he was frightened. Some weeks later I went to check an item in the property and as I was flicking through pages, I notice a starting pistol. I do not know why it leapt out at me but it did and on checking I saw it had been booked in on the same day as the 'cell shooting'; it had also been booked in by one of the detectives who had been in the cells.

I went to see the same Chief Superintendent who had spoken to me at the time of the incident. His message was to let things drop. He told me that there was no complainant and no proof that any gun had been fired. Once again, I could not believe this was happening but within weeks the original complainant had given a statement saying nothing had happened and he had made everything up. To this day I remain convinced that the gun was used, I heard the bang and I saw a tearful prisoner on his hands and knees. Make your own mind up!

Most of the time working in the Charge Office was fairly mundane, though every now and then something happened that had us all racing around in a panic. One of the most frequent annoyances was when prisoners got their heads stuck in the cell doors. The doors were large, heavy metal structures with a small round window and a hatch. The hatch was for passing food and drinks into the cell and was supposed to be closed at all other times. Prisoners, however, liked the hatches open so that they could talk to their neighbours and to hear better they would push their heads through the hatches. It seemed easy to push heads out but more difficult to get them back again.

On several occasions we had to use Vaseline or butter in an effort to free heads and once even that did not work. The Fire Brigade had to be called and the cell door was removed from its hinges. As the door and prisoner were laid in a horizontal position the unwilling captive passed out. It took nearly an hour to free him and we had a doctor in attendance for most of that time. I was not at all pleased with my warder and had told him many times to shut the hatches but he was not alone and within weeks another door had to be removed on a different shift.

No picture of life in a Charge Office would be complete without a mention of the smell and general lack of hygiene. I have read that submariners always comment on the smell of their environment and it was the same for us. The mixture of smells could be truly horrendous. None of the individual smells such as sweat, flatulence, stale alcohol and rancid socks could be termed pleasant, but add them all together in a continuously warm atmosphere and the results were numbing. Some days it was so bad that you could still detect the odour on your clothes when you got home.

We had ventilators and blowers and all sorts of technology but none of it seemed to make any difference. Further, while I was working there fan assisted ovens were introduced to heat the prisoner's food. This process wafted blasts of warm, food related smells along the cell corridors. The food was often of a reasonable quality but as days went by one food smell was overlaid on another.

Germs must have been rife in that sweaty miasma of odours. The doctor was a regular visitor, though he was usually called by prisoners who were drug dependent and found themselves doing 'cold turkey' in the cells. We also had outbreaks of ring worm, flea infestations, scabies and various other diseases. You just could not think of it or you would become paranoid. Just before I moved on, AIDS was starting to become known and we were issued warnings about avoiding contact with blood. Some prisoners played on this and often self-harmed so as to smear their cells in blood. A really wonderful environment in which to work.

I had just settled in when the Chief Constable called me and told me I was being promoted to inspector. I was delighted, but my main thought was "up you George Henry". I had survived and was back on track.

CHAPTER SIXTEEN

'SIR.'

My new station was over forty miles from anywhere I had worked before. It was both a wrench and at the same time a welcome chance of a new beginning. It felt good to have Bath Stars, or pips, of the inspectors' insignia on my shoulders.

The station was another old building. At either side of a squat, rectangular block was an ornate red brick house frontage. The house to the left had originally been the Superintendents' house but now provided offices for all the officer classes who worked from the building. The right-hand house held the CID and the station's administration. All other ranks and offices were housed in the rectangular block. Everywhere seemed cramped and people were wedged into offices like sardines into a can. In spite of the congestion the station had a large licensed bar and a massive snooker room, both of which were very well used.

There was a strong sense of history to my new place of work. Until ten years earlier it had belonged to a different Police Force and some of the officers still did not believe that times had moved on. At the first local Football Match that I worked on I noticed that two officers still had metal badges that belonged to the old Force. They were detectives who were working in uniform for overtime but the fact that this could happen was uncanny. Many weeks later the Force sold a police house that was surplus to requirements. I was on duty after the sale when a call was received from the new owner. He asked if I could visit him at what was now his house. When I did so he opened the garage and there was an old Police car bearing the insignia of a Force that handed the area over years before.

How no one noticed that there was a car in the garage for over ten years was beyond me However, as the quirky, strangeness of my new place of work became evident I ceased to be surprised.

The station had its own control room and custody office. The overall commander was a superintendent and his deputy, a chief inspector called Sharon, was highly visible at everything that went on. She made me feel nervous, she addressed me strangely. "Now then flower you just pop along and do that little job for me, there's a darling". I suppose that she was doing no more than women complain men do all the time. I liked her, she was an extremely competent officer and she always made it very clear what she wanted doing.

My sergeants were excellent, though in retrospect they were probably at the station to be kept out of the way. Dyson Malpas was a huge man with a shock of white hair and dark sunken eyes. His first impression on me was that he could provoke fear with a look. He was almost identical to the large cop in Charlie Chaplin's film, 'The Kid'. If you never saw that film then just think Hagrid from Harry Potter but with bleached hair.

Dyson had been a detective but had fallen out with the senior officers at his last station. He liked a drink and I was told to 'watch him' when briefed by the superintendent on my arrival. Within a week the advice seemed to have been good. Dyson was 'off sick' and I decided to visit him. He was living with a very respectable lady in a pleasant area. The night before he had gone sick, he went drinking. The hours and pints drifted one into another until Dyson realized his partner would be furious that he was so late. He staggered home and found the house in darkness. Somewhere, he had a key but he failed to find it and he decided to climb in through the upstairs bedroom window rather than start banging at the door. Somehow, he managed to scale the wall and get the window open far enough to climb in.

At this stage things went wrong. Dyson had forgotten that just inside the window was a rack holding plants, some of which were cacti. As he fell into the bedroom, he ended up sat in a pile of upturned plant pots. His bottom was a pin cushion of cacti spines. When I was allowed upstairs on my visit, he was lying with his bare bottom pointing at the ceiling. It was very red and swollen.

Less than a week later Dyson asked to leave work early one Saturday afternoon. I let him go without giving it much thought. About three hours later the constable from the control room told me that he had received a phone call from his daughter. She had told him that, "that nice sergeant Malpas was asleep on a bench in the bus station". He was apparently wearing his uniform so I set off with another sergeant to find him. He was exactly as described, snoring loudly and stinking of beer. Fortunately, although he had his uniform on, he had a jacket over the top. We took him home and deposited him safely inside.

A week later he asked for time off again so I decided I would go with him to see what happened. As a rugby player I was certain I could match Dyson if he was drinking beer. After a fairly heavy drinking session I saw my sergeant into a taxi and then got one myself. I was supposed to be going out later and decided to watch television for a while. When I woke up my underpants were on fire! I had taken my uniform trousers off and laid on the rug in front of the gas fire. I felt totally disoriented and vowed never to drink with Dyson again.

When we first worked nights together, I found something else about him. There was a Wharfe just outside the town and a Danish ship was supposed to be preparing for sea. Unfortunately, the captain found that he had unwelcome guests on board. Most of its crew had returned to the ship with female company. Money had changed hands and all sorts of sexual escapades had taken place. Now the sailors were unwilling to give up their 'ladies' and they, in turn, showed no sign of wanting to leave.

We were called to escort the prostitutes off the ship. It had the potential to go badly wrong. The crew were drunk, the women undressed and the ships' accommodation was confined. As we clambered down a flight of stairs two rough looking men stumbled towards us holding iron bars. Dyson moved towards them, trying to take his truncheon out. Then I heard a female voice,

"Dyson. Hey Sheila it's that nice Sergeant you like. Show us your truncheon, Dyson!"

The owner of the voice was a skinny woman with bottled blonde hair. She was sat on a toilet with her nickers round her ankles and her tattooed breasts on total display. Once again, I had heard Dyson referred to as nice. This time it was clear that he was friends with all the prostitutes and the situation was quickly calmed down.

The ship sailed and Dyson conveyed a van load of barely dressed prostitutes to various parts of the town. Within an hour of returning to the station I had him back in the van. I intended to give him no chance to make up a story as to how he knew the girls. No sooner had we driven out of the station yard than a transit van mounted the kerb in front of us and crashed into a garden wall. We pulled up behind it and approached the van. The driver appeared comatose, slumped over the steering wheel he was, however, breathing. We went to check the extent of the damage and as we did so the van engine, which we had switched off, was restarted. The driver reversed back onto the road, narrowly missing passing traffic and he roared off away from us. We decided to try and catch him. Nowadays 'chases' by ordinary police officers are outlawed. You can call them 'pursuits' but the point is you are following safely not trying to catch an offender. On that night we quickly realized we would have to do more than follow. The van driver was taking every corner fully on the wrong side of the road. It was only a matter of time before he hit someone head on.

After a few minutes we had the chance to pull alongside the van and I managed to force it off the road and into a wooded area where it collided with a tree. The impact between the vehicles had been minimal but damage was noticeable. The driver was arrested and found to be so far over the drink drive alcohol limit that he had to be hospitalized. I was suspended from driving and Dyson announced that the incident had convinced him he no longer wanted to be a police officer!

Several months passed and Dyson seemed to have settled down. Then one day as I sat in my office catching up on paperwork a strange individual arrived at the station. Until this visitor arrived, I had never seen a bowler hat outside of London. The man was short, balding with a little salt and pepper moustache. He was immaculately dressed and he reminded me of George Smiley, the John Le Carre character.

From his briefcase the visitor produced a sheaf of papers. These turned out to be an application form that had been completed by Dyson. I had no knowledge of his pursuing a job but I remembered the night of the transit van.

The visitor asked me questions about Dysons' capabilities, reliability, use of language and ability to handle difficult situations. He seemed to like my answers and explained that the job application was for a post in Embassy Security. Dyson could find himself anywhere in the world where Her Majesty's Government had an Embassy. I was then asked if Dyson liked to drink?

I felt trapped. Do Fish live in water? Does day follow night? Does Dyson Malpas like a drink? What to say? That was the question. So, I lied. I said I had never seen Dyson the worse for drink, that he liked a social drink but usually looked after others who could not handle alcohol. He was a reputable pillar of the establishment. He was so good he got the job and I lost a sergeant and a little colour went out of the World.

My other 'outside' sergeant was much less of an extrovert. The problem with him was that he did not like to go out of the station. He was widely recognized as an 'Olympic Flame' and this created problems in providing supervision to the constables. He was a master at finding reasons to stop inside the station and there was always a cupboard or a drawer that he felt needed tidying.

I decided to get him out more and soon after I arrived, I told him that I would go out with him. He expected that we would have a tour in a patrol car but I told him we were walking. We walked miles and he seemed to be limping when we returned. Later I went into the control room and there was the sergeant sat on a stool with his trousers rolled and his feet in a bowl of warm water. He was hobbling for days but he did make an effort to get out and about.

I quickly seemed to settle into this new environment. One event seemed to lead to another and my out and about style seemed to go down well with the constables. One night I decided to go for a jog during my meal break and I took a radio in case anything happened. As I trotted along, I heard the control room sergeant pass on the details of a wanted person. A constable thought he had seen the person in question within the last few minutes so I changed the direction of my jog. Within five minutes I saw a man answering the description and I called for assistance. I then ran up behind the man and told him that he was under arrest. He immediately set off running and I pursued him until he suddenly stopped and turned to face me. For a brief moment I thought he wanted to fight and then he held his hands out in submission. A patrol car arrived and we escorted the man into the station.

The custody sergeant looked strangely at me as I walked in wearing a pair of running shorts and a vest The man looked totally bemused and before he was asked anything he said,

"I've been arrested loads of time but never by a fucking Batman in silk shorts."

For several weeks my officers were referring to me as Batman and I was not keen to change the nickname. However, I was not as keen on my next name. When I had gone to Bramshill I had needed a reliable car and I decided to buy a brand-new Lada. I received a lot of flak from my colleagues who believed driving a Russian car was somehow not the done thing. I travelled thousands of miles in that car and it just kept going week after week. The door handles fell off, the plastic cover on the dashboard fell off and the gear lever knob fell off but the engine was sound. I had decided that I wanted something a little more up market and, in a moment of madness, I bought a Reliant Scimitar.

My new car was a black, three litre Sports car and I loved it. At least I loved it on the days that it actually worked. It cost me a fortune in repairs but that was not the real problem. The registered number began WWW and quite quickly a constable christened me 'Wee Willie Winkey'. I preferred Batman but I was stuck with the new name.

The sub division that I was working at was located alongside an estuary. There was a small shopping centre and then there was a long promenade that flanked the river. Holiday makers turned up in droves. The inland side of the promenade was fully built up. There were Hotels, houses, Fish and Chip shops, Chinese Take Aways and pub after pub. The whole promenade resembled the Wild West. There were brawls, drunken nuisance, damage to property and regular anti-social behaviour. In spite of the number of complaints made by residents there were few people arrested.

I thought that some of my constables were a little lazy. I spent hours walking along the promenade but eventually became aware that I had not seen anything. All the reports came from the landward side of the promenade. That side was packed with parked cars, many of them were double parked, some were abandoned on the footpath and you could not see what was happening beyond the cars.

I decided to use a little lateral thinking. My constables were not able to arrest offenders because they could not see them. The answer was to target the vehicles that obstructed our view. I got a large batch of tickets for parking and vehicle offences. I informed my officers to be very obvious in their approach and let residents see what was happening.

On the first night we issued sixty tickets. That was more than the whole sub division had managed to get rid of in a month. On the next night we issued seventy! The station was bombarded with complaints by many people who had received tickets. The Clerk of the Justices contacted the superintendent to advise him of the work we were causing for his courts. Gradually the parking situation improved and we were able to see what was happening along the promenade and the number of arrests increased dramatically.

In the coming weeks the number of incidents that the public reported decreased. I know that some incidents were displaced to side streets but the quality of life improved. The older inspectors did not agree with my approach, but they did eventually support the efforts of my staff.

I was really happy to be making a difference and was able to work closely with my officers. Unfortunately, events were to take a course beyond my control.

CHAPTER SEVENTEEN

THE MINERS' STRIKE

Margaret Thatcher, as Prime Minister, had taken on Argentina to protect British Sovereignty over the Falkland Islands. She had defeated a country who had been presented as our attackers. The strategy was bold, perhaps even reckless, but it came off, thousands of miles from the United Kingdom.

Galtieri as the Dictator of Argentina was presented as an archetypal villain and the majority of our population supported Thatcher's actions. The successful outcome of the campaign catapulted Thatcher to a position of immense political power. She had defeated external enemies and took advantage of her position to launch an industrial strategy against the coal miners.

Her intention was to bring about a wholesale closure of pits and to defeat the power of the National Union of Miners. She regarded coal as a historic fuel and realized that imported coal would be cheaper than most English mines could produce. The leader of the NUM, Arthur Scargill, was steeped in Communist politics and he believed that mines should be kept open at any cost so that jobs would be preserved. Thatcher branded Scargill as 'the enemy within."

On the sixth of March, 1984, Arthur Scargill called his members out on strike. He had taken up the challenge which the Prime Minister had presented to him. The cards were stacked against Scargill and the Yorkshire Miners and he had stepped into a trap.

The Yorkshire pits went on strike just as winter came to an end. Thatcher had ensured that huge stocks of fuel were held in reserve. She had also organized the police well before the NUM walked out. The Police opened the National Reporting Centre which created a system of mutual support between Forces. The Chief Constable of Humberside took over command of the centre and ran an almost militaristic campaign.

Scargill hoped that he would prevent the movement of coal and secure the closure of all the pits by using 'Flying Pickets'. The Yorkshire miners would travel around the country and ensure there was total 'support' for the strike. They also sought to prevent fuel reaching steel works and power stations. The Police stopped the travelling pickets to prevent breaches of the peace.

The miners in the Midlands and pits in other parts continued to work. The strike did not have a national mandate and Scargill dare not call a ballot of all miners. The strike was unofficial and, therefore, other unions did not strike in support. In July of 1984 forty percent of the public supported the employers and thirty three percent supported the miners. By December fifty one percent supported the employers and only twenty six percent supported the miners. A tragedy was unfolding day by day as an industry and a community failed to realize that their time was up.

At the time I lost sight of what the bigger picture was. I am sure that most officers switched off to anything other than counting the money they were earning. We worked endless hours and became zombies, sent from one place to another. I will tell you some of the events that took place stripped of the suffering that the miners experienced. In some ways we were victims ourselves as our lives became suspended.

I was sent to a Territorial Army Barracks which had been taken over to provide a rest centre and feeding area for police officers. There were some periods when the barracks held over two hundred officers. Some arrived in the morning and remained there until teatime. Others came for a couple of hours before being despatched to a particular location. All of them needed feeding and providing with warm drinks.

Some of the officers slept in their vans for several hours, others lounged around the barracks hall, some read, many played cards for high stakes. Eventually the Metropolitan Officers secured a supply of pornographic films. There was very little trouble at the barracks, though the Met officers needed close watching. Their vans were loaded with bags of potatoes, cabbages, eggs and fresh fish. The weight of the vans increased dramatically just before they returned to London.

On one occasion we had a hundred Met officers who were sent to the local wharfe to ensure the unloading of imported coal. As soon as the vans left a sense of peace and quiet descended on the barracks. Only an hour later my assistant came to tell me that we did not have enough chairs for the next arrival. I knew we had had hundreds of chairs so I checked the building, there were under a hundred left.

I took one of the local Force vans and drove out to the wharfe. The sun was shining as I drove through the countryside and eventually arrived at the wharfe. The Met officers were sat along the banks of the estuary, some of them had stretched themselves between two chairs. All of them were in various stages of undress. Most of them had taken their shirts off, some were in shirt sleeves with their trousers rolled up. I radioed for some assistance and we then recovered one hundred and thirty chairs that the Met had 'acquired'.

There was no sign of any pickets but the Met resembled a large invading army that local residents were extremely wary off. I was pleased when they set off home. The Met also arrived at other holding centres and they were also provided with overnight accommodation. I was glad that the barracks under my charge had no night-time accommodation. In Nottingham the Met were confined to their base on a night. They were forbidden to leave the premises and denied the use of their vehicles. One group decided to abscond for a night in the pub and on returning they crashed into a bridge.

The officers then returned to their accommodation, took the number plates off another van along with the vehicle identification plate and placed those on the smashed van. They then took over the undamaged van and fitted their number plates and VIN to it. They may have been imaginative but they were caught out within twenty-four hours.

Shortly after the recovery of the chairs I was sat in the office at the barracks. My assistant was also working away at keeping a record of officers who had passed through the holding centre. Suddenly there was a sharp rap at the door followed immediately by the door opening. An army sergeant marched in, drew himself to attention and saluted me.

"I have got representatives of the Press for you, Sir".

He then turned and marched out before entering again with two men in long raincoats.

"These men is from the 'News of the World', Sir."

I was suddenly posed with a large problem. The News of the World were renowned for featuring scandalous stories and I knew that Force policy stated that I should refer their questions to our press office. However, the two men stood there, armed with pens and notebooks, one of them also had a camera.

"How can I help you?" I asked.

'We've had a phone call telling us that police officers are having orgies here on a night. What is going on here at night."

I could not see a problem in answering.

"I can tell you that there are no police officers here on a night. They all go to residential bases by seven in the evening and we hand the keys back to the army until the following morning."

"Where are the beds then? Asked the older reporter.

"Look, there are no beds here. I can show you round."

So, I escorted the reporters round the Barracks Hall and the cinema room.

"Are there any women here?" Asked the younger reporter.

"I can only remember about a dozen female officers being here at any time. There are no typists or secretaries. I do not know who or what has caused the report. I suppose it may have been a miner, but I do not know."

Both reporters were thankful for having been shown round. They said they would do a report on the police organization and they promised to let our press office see it before it was published. I felt a total sense of relief as they left the building. I was happy that there had been nothing untoward and I went for a walk round the site.

As I skirted round the perimeter the grounds, I saw a car parked across the road. A man was sat in the driving seat staring at the barracks. I then returned to the building and as I came into the office, I saw my assistant embracing and kissing the cleaner. I was not only shocked by the brazenness after the visit of the reporters but I also realized exactly what had caused the report to the press.

The cleaner saw me and adjusted her clothes before scurrying out of the office leaving a smell of cheap perfume and sweat.

"I'm sorry, Sir......"

"I suppose this has been going on for a few nights then". I asked.

"Yes, Sir, the husband will have suspected. We never did it outside. We just had a bang in here before I locked up."

"I suggest that you ask your boss if you can go back to usual duties."

"Well, I don't want to do that. I work twelve hours a day and get a rest day on pay every week. I like this job. I want to stay."

"I think it would benefit everyone if you moved on. You have had sex while on duty, so the job has paid you for doing that. You have compromised our position here and opened the door to let a domestic dispute explode in our faces. You should do the decent thing."

He shuffled from foot to foot then agreed that he would leave.

"Three days until you move, OK?"

"Yes, Sir."

I had liked the job myself. There were plenty of logistic issues to deal with, it was warm, there was no heavy paperwork to deal with. Also, the food was free and excellent. I went to the local police canteen and the cooks used to ask me what I wanted. I had steak, fresh fish, roast potatoes, strawberries and ice cream. Strangely my tenure at the barracks was concluded before my assistants ended. I was asked to go back to my subdivision and lead the team that had been committed to the frontline against the miners. So, I was about to enter the real world.

On my first morning I was due at work for five am. I left home at four o clock, it was dark and cold and not a vehicle on the road as I drove to work. I entered the station car park and two transit vans already had their engines running. Some officers were already in the vans and fast asleep, others were in the station drinking tea or coffee.

At five we drove out of the car park and set off towards South Yorkshire. The inside of the van soon became hot, many officers were comatose and some snoring loudly. There was a regular sound of breaking wind followed by a stench similar to rotting vegetation. The atmosphere inside the vans was a miasma of warm, damp, putridness.

We drove to a roundabout near the border with South Yorkshire and informed the reporting centre that we were in position. Then we sat there and waited and waited. Most of the officers remained asleep as dawn broke and the sun rose. We watched vehicles pass us and looked out for miners, we saw nothing untoward. After four hours we were sent to a nearby café and were provided with a cooked English breakfast and vast quantities of coffee.

Then we went to another junction and sat there for another four hours before we were sent to another café for a cooked meal. We were also supplied with 'Max Packs'. Those were ready drinks that just needed hot water being added. Finally, we were sent back to our station where we arrived sixteen hours after having set off. That was eight hours overtime and some of the officers could tell you how much they earned per minute!

I went home, fell asleep on my settee and woke up just after midnight and only four hours before I had to get up. This became the daily routine. Life was suspended.

The days merged one into another. I can remember particular events among a whole lot of mundane days. The first dramatic episode that we experienced began just the same as any other day. We were instructed to drive to a Haulage Company Depot and to ensure that the premises and vehicles there were protected from travelling pickets.

The depot was located on a large industrial estate. It was surrounded by a high fence and only had one wide gate. Inside the enclosed area was a block of offices, a block of porta toilets and a large, low building that provided rest facilities for the company's drivers. There were a dozen lorries parked in two lines.

My constables moved into the drivers rest room, unloaded their ready drinks and biscuits. They turned the heaters up and many of them immediately went to sleep. I walked round the perimeter with one of my sergeants, we could see no movement outside the depot. In fact, we saw no one and no vehicles. I had two constables standing at the gate and after two hours they were replaced by another pair. The sun came up and a number of the officers became restless.

Four hours after we arrived, I was told to send one van to a feeding centre. That left eight constables, a sergeant and myself. Shortly afterwards a few drivers arrived and waited for instructions to go and collect coal. Then a number of cars arrived and parked up some hundred yards away. Men got out of the cars and collected in a group. Eventually there were about fifty men who seemed to be under the control of a tall man with a loud hailer.

It was obvious that we were facing miners and we informed the control centre. We closed the gate and lined the officers up on the inside of the depot. Suddenly the men ran along the road towards the gate. They were shouting, some carried pieces of wood and stones. It was quite frightening. As they approached, they hurled stones over the fence which clattered off the lorries and buildings. One or two windows were smashed. Very little hit us as the stones flew over us or hit the fence. The men then grabbed the metal fence and began pulling and tugging at it. The supports bent towards them but did not give.

There is little doubt that we would have been given a good hiding if the miners had got into the depot. Then we heard a rumble like thunder and the miners let go of the fence and seemed to be listening to the noise. We realised that we were actually hearing the sound of truncheons being beaten on laminate shields. Then a contingent of Public Order Police from the Greater Manchester Force entered the street that led to the depot. They were fully equipped with protective kit and they marched forward in ordered lines. The miners were trapped against the fence as the Manchester officers advanced passed the parked cars. Then the officers started to run still in lines, the miners started towards them, then some tried to escape sideways while others attempted to climb the fence.

The Manchester officers attacked the miners like a violent wave, truncheons fell on heads, shoulders and arms. As the miners fell, they were kicked by heavy boots and some were trampled on. Then the arrest process began as beaten and stricken miners were hauled away. We never opened the gate, none of the Manchester officers spoke to us. Some of the miners escaped to their cars and roared off. There was blood on the footpath outside the depot.

The lorries then departed to collect coal for a steel works. They thanked us profusely even though we had done next to nothing. My other van load of officers returned and could not believe they had missed the action. They were keen to tell us how bad the food had been. The bacon had thick rind on it with hairs protruding from the rind. The sausages looked like decomposing fingers that tasted high and had green herbs in them which gave them an even more sinister appearance. There was nothing left for us, so we were told to get sandwiches from a supermarket, which to me was a relief.

Then we settled down until the lorries returned, at which time we were told to return to our station. We had been there for ten hours and half of us had deployed for twenty minutes. That did not seem the best way to spend a day and so the strike continued along its course of attrition.

Most of the time we had little contact with miners, and even less often did we get to communicate with them. Just once was there a real connection with the suffering strikers. We had been sent to watch a back road into Scunthorpe and we parked up on the car park at the front of a pub. We sat there for three hours and eventually we were delivered enough sandwiches to feed a whole Police Division. Hardly a car had passed our position let alone strikers. We were told that there were miners in the area and we were strongly told to remain where we were.

As we walked round the car park, we suddenly realized that a number of men were watching us from the pub. One of them held up a hand written banner, 'The Miners united will never be defeated.'. For a moment I thought hostilities were about to start. I decided to go into the pub and there in the Lounge were eight men spread round the room.

"Now then Lads. How long have you been here?" I asked.

"We've been here since you got here. We've been watching you!"

"Where are you going then."

"Well, we'll wait till things quiet down in Yorkshire and then go home. There's nowt happening here."

"How are you doing? "I asked.

"We are bloody starving," answered one of the miners.

I sent out to the van and got all the spare sandwiches sent in. They were attacked by the ravenous miners and I apologized to the landlord. After they'd eaten, the miners came out and chatted with our officers. It was a weird experience and we never saw them again. They drove off. We reported that they had gone towards Yorkshire and we were told to go home.

A few mornings later we were sent to Scunthorpe again. As usual the vans were lined up for departure at four thirty am. The officers were largely the same group that I had together for over two months. They were all so used to the routine that they operated like robots. The atmosphere in the vans was as unpleasant as it always was but no one grumbled any more. Then about half way to our destination there was a thud and an exclamation from the back of the van.

I looked over my shoulder and saw one of the more mature officers bleeding from his nose.

"What's happened.?" I asked.

No one said anything.

"Right, be sure to tell me when we get there."

We drove on in silence and most of them drifted off to sleep again. Our task was to secure the steel works to the north of Scunthorpe. There were about five gates and we would drop off two officers at each gate. The two vans would then move from gate to gate to let the officers sit down for a while.

As we stopped at the first gate, I instructed the first two officers to disembark and check their radios. We then moved to the next gate and let the next two get out. So, it continued. At the last gate I instructed two officers to take up their positions.

"I can't get out Sir."

"Can you tell me why you can't get out?" I asked.

"It's embarrassing Sir."

"Either get out or explain."

"Well, I'm in my sleeping bag Sir. I've only just realized what's happened."

"Go on."

"Well, I got to the station a bit late. I took my boots and trousers off so I could get in the sleeping bag. I took them off at the back of the van. I think they're still there in the station carpark. I'm sorry Sir."

So, the constable had travelled in his uniform top, his underpants and his socks. I only had one option I told the driver to take the trouser less officers' post. I then had the part dressed man take over driving in his underpants. That seemed the line of least resistance, however, the situation soon got worse.

"I need to tell you what happened, Boss." Said the new driver.

You know Steve Evans is an ex-sailor. Well, he shoved his hand in my sleeping bag and grabbed my cock. So, I thumped him. What would you do?"

"Are you sure his hand was inside your sleeping bag?" I asked.

"I'm sure he did that. I know he squeezed my cock."

"Do you think anyone else saw him lean across and shove his hand in your sleeping bag. I know he wasn't sat next to you."

"Well, someone put their hand in my bag and I just know that Steve Evans is a queer. It must have been him."

"What do you want me to do?"

"I want to move to another sub division. I don't want to be where he is. Otherwise, I'm going to complain about him."

"Look I'll try and sort this out back at the station. I can't deal with that here because I cannot see him and you together. Especially with you in your underpants."

That was it for the rest of the day. Back at the station I saw Constable Evans and he had a very different story. He said that some officers had always suggested he was homosexual because he had been at sea. He was heterosexual, he was married with two kids. He had leaned across and shaken the complainant to ask if he had a newspaper. The officer sat next to the man in the sleeping bag then put his hand in the bag to wake him up. Evans said he had never touched inside the bag. Further, if anyone said he did then he wanted to complain that he had been assaulted.

What a mess. I took the easy way out and passed the investigation to Discipline and Complaints. The case was resolved pragmatically. The trouser less man was moved at his request but he was told there would be less overtime opportunities. PC Evans was exonerated, after the officer who had been sat next to the complainant said he had put his hand in the sleeping bag to provoke a reaction. The 'grabber' was put on control room duties and was also unable to work overtime. Rough justice all round I suppose and I guess the thought of someone leaving their trousers on the car park was a little amusing.

I also embarrassed myself as the strike dragged on week after week. One evening I arrived home at about seven o' clock. I remember laying on my settee and then I must have drifted off into a deep sleep. Suddenly I woke up not really sure where I was. It was daylight and I saw a milkman across the road. Children were also walking past my house. I looked at my watch and saw that it was quarter to nine and I believed that I was nearly three hours late for work. I jumped up from the settee and ran to the phone. I rang the control room and told them that I would drive straight to the steelworks where my unit was deployed.

The control sergeant accepted what I had told him and after I had put the phone down, I went to get a clean shirt. As I came downstairs the phone rang. The sergeant was now ringing me and he seemed amused by what was going on. After a brief chat he told me that I should go to bed. It was not the morning after all. I had only been at home for an hour and three quarters. The milkman was collecting payment not delivering and the night was light with it being early August.

My heart was pounding and although I was shattered, I could not sleep. I had lost all sense of time. The following morning, I was up before five am and early at work. We drove to the steelworks and deployed at the gates as usual. After a time, we were instructed to leave the gates and move out of sight from the road. It was felt that we were overreacting in the absence of any pickets.

The border of the steelworks was marked by a raised embankment. We parked behind it and could not be seen by the public. After a time, officers laid on the grass and took the opportunity to get some sleep. The radio was absolutely silent and we were gradually lulled into a false sense of security so we decided to have an impromptu cricket match using a pallet as a wicket, a short plank as a bat and a rolled-up ball of paper cello taped together.

After playing for an hour, I took my shirt off and lay down with some of the officers. Once again, I fell fast asleep. I woke up at one stage to notice that some wise guy had drawn two 'pips' (bath stars) on top of my shoulders. Just at this point three officers in full uniform marched over the embankment. Two of the officers were traffic constables but the one in the middle was an Assistant Chief Constable. We were caught out in full relaxation mode.

I heard the ACC ask an officer who was in charge and as I started to get up. I heard the reply clearly.

"Don't you know the insignia of an inspector. That's him with the pips."

I wished the earth would have swallowed us up as the ACC made his way towards me.

"Are you following the summer dress code?" He asked.

There was no clear answer and we were fortunate that this Chief Officer had a sense of humour. I am sure he must have realized that this group of officers were about at the end of their tether. None of them would have given up the opportunity of earning overtime but the break had been necessary.

The strike continued for another seven months but I cannot remember anything specific from this point onwards. I do remember watching a violent episode at Orgreave. There were about five thousand miners and the same number of officers. I watched it taking place on TV and got a clear impression of public opinion about the strike. As mounted police officers charged the miners, working men in the pub applauded the police. For the miners the writing was already on the wall, their industry was in its' death throw. I could not bring myself to regard the end of the strike as a victory I could only celebrate the fact that we could try and return to normality. Whatever that was!

I enjoyed working for my new superintendent. I had been at his station for months but we had seldom met. He was a stickler for discipline but he was a fair man. He was a member of the Salvation Army and applied his Christian faith in dealing with his staff. He also turned out whenever a serious incident took place. When two off duty police officers went missing whilst fishing in the estuary he turned out and took command. He called in mounted police, the diving section, every special constable he could call upon and he waded through the deep, sticky mud with the rest of us. He also conveyed the sad news to the officers' relatives when their drowned bodies were found.

I did have one little altercation with the superintendent. My Scimitar had broken down one Saturday and I took it into a local garage. The proprietor who became a good friend told me I could borrow a complimentary car while he worked on mine. The car turned out to be a Citroen 2 CV. It was sparkly pink in colour with a ban the bomb logo on the boot lid. The windows had anarchy stickers and Green Peace posters. I went to work on Sunday and parked in the covered garage that was used by the superintendent. The garage was seldom used on a Sunday so I thought I was safe but the car had only been there for a few hours when I got a phone call from the superintendent who told me to get a criminal's car out of the car park. When I told him it was mine, at least temporarily, he lectured me on standards and insisted it was inappropriate.

He never mentioned it again. On another occasion, however, I believe that his dogmatic approach left him as something of a joke. He was adamant that officers should wear headgear at all times. On one occasion he turned up at a football match that I was in charge of. The crowd was around five thousand and we had some fifty officers on duty in and outside the ground.

I had briefed everyone and instructed them not to appear without helmets or caps on. I was in the football control box with a radio operator, a spotter to watch out for known troublemakers and a sergeant. About twenty minutes before kick off the superintendent arrived on a surprise visit. Everything seemed under control and I got him a cup of coffee, then suddenly he went red and seemed about to explode.

"Get that man here," he almost shouted.

I could see an officer in shirt sleeves walking down the far touchline. I asked the spotter for his binoculars and focused on the officer. It was a sergeant, not wearing any headgear. However, I recognized the man, he was a referee as well as a policeman.

"I think that's the referee, Sir" I stated.

"I don't care who he is. Get him here."

Now we had less than quarter of an hour before kick-off. The referee would brief his linesmen and give instructions to the teams. He also was due to discuss arrangements with me in his changing room. So, I went.

I explained that the superintendent wanted to see him but he declined as he had started work as a referee and was authorized to do that by the Force. I returned to the box and informed the superintendent that the referee was not coming and as I conveyed that message the officials walked onto the pitch ahead of the teams. For a moment I thought the superintendent was about to go onto the pitch and get him but at the last-minute sanity held sway.

Years before I led my officers during the Miners' Strike, I had faced a gun for the first time. I was patrolling the streets of the city when a landlord called the Police to his pub. I attended with another constable who had previously been a sergeant in the regular army. The landlord told us that he had evacuated the pub, leaving a single man armed with a gun sat in the premises. I guess we should have called firearms officers but my colleague marched through the front door as if he was a sheriff entering a Wild West saloon. It was a long narrow pub and the lone man was sat at the far end of the floor space. We walked towards him.

As we approached the man he suddenly leapt to his feet and picked a pistol up off the table. He raised his hand and aimed at us. My life flashed in front of me and the stupidity of entering unarmed seemed to slap me in the face. The man made a strange gurgling noise and then said something like "Bang". My colleague spoke to him and the gunman gurgled again with a broad grin on his face and it became clear to me that he was mute. I asked him to put the gun down and he did with no hesitation. He was harmless and the gun was a replica Colt

Peacemaker. We walked him out of the pub and took him to the station where he was eventually collected by Social Services. The ending had been successful but I never wanted to see a gun again.

Then, one weekend, as an inspector, I found myself facing a gun again and leading officers in dangerous circumstances. At that time, I had had no training in dealing with Firearms incidents and I almost messed that up as well. The day had been very quiet when we were called to a man on the roof of a garage within fifty meters of the station. He turned out to have a shotgun and he had aimed it at people who were passing by along the footpath. I was told that this was the son of a serving police officer who owned the house to which the garage was attached. He clearly had a grievance against his father and he was demanding his father come and face him.

I sent two officers to the street at the back of the house and I positioned myself and two officers behind a van across the road. The distance from the man with the shotgun to us was less than thirty meters and I had placed us all in danger. I had the ends of the street closed to vehicles and pedestrians and I asked for a Firearms Commander.

As we waited, one of the officers with me told us what a strange man the father was. He seldom acted as a police officer and operated his police car as a grocer's delivery service rather than what he was paid for. Fairly recently he had skidded on the ice in a rural village and the road was littered with eggs, tinned vegetables and sundry other items. The inside of the car was also full of chickens and slices of ham. He managed to talk himself out of his business dealings by saying he helped rural communities get by!

In spite of this knowledge neither officer knew what had caused this explosive incident. As we began to shout to the gunman and ask if he wanted anything, a car burst through the tape at the end of the road. As the car, a Volvo, approached us its' exhaust dropped off and the noise was horrendous. It stopped right in front of us and in line of fire of the gunman. The driver got out and I recognized him as a Firearms Commander. He turned his back on us and walked towards the garage where the gunman was now quite agitated.

Ten minutes later the commander walked towards us with the gun and the young man who had been on the roof of the garage. It was over and the commander was quite complimentary of what I had done. For my part I thought he had been reckless but maybe he had a second sense for judging situations or it may have been the exhaust falling off that set the scene.

My car was also in a terrible state and I was travelling to work on a Honda 50 or sometimes jogging to the station from home. I had been recommended J K Autos and I had been very impressed when I took my Scimitar there. John Kelly was a character who became part of my life over the next two years. He was married to a woman from a wealthy family and he had set up his garage as an all singing service centre. He had mechanics, bodyworkers, sprayers, recovery and complimentary vehicles. The garage had the floor space of a football pitch.

John was ruggedly good looking but did have a resemblance of Fred Dibnah, the man who used to blow up chimneys on TV. He often went out in his blue overalls with oil and grease up to his elbows. However, he also rode in the local hunt and moved among the upper echelons of society. We got on well from the outset, though his actions often worried me as he sailed close to the illegal.

When I took my Scimitar in, John said that he did not have a car that he could loan me while he worked on it. He then rang me and said that I could borrow his car for a few days and when I went to collect it, I was amazed. The vehicle he was offering me was a grey Aston Martin sports car. It wasn't new but it was almost pristine. I was worried about scratching it or damaging it in any way but he just laughed that off and sent me on my way reassured that I was covered on his insurance.

The following day I went for a drive on rural roads and ended up calling for lunch in a pub. The landlord was friendly enough and I thought that was because I was his only customer. Half way through my meal a smart man in a tweed jacket came in and chatted with the landlord before leaving as quickly as he had arrived. I finished my meal, ordered a coffee and was about to leave when the man in tweed returned with two police officers.

The policemen asked if the car was mine and I immediately said it was not. They asked where I had got it from and I told them it belonged to John Kelly. Only then did the man identify himself as the owner and said that he had taken it to JK'S Garage for a service. Fortunately, they rang the garage and John arrived about half an hour later. There was a slightly heated exchange between the tweed jacketed man and John before things ended amicably. It was agreed that I could keep the vehicle for the next twenty-four hours and John said he would service it free of charge. My relief was almost total, though the exhilaration of driving an Aston faded quickly at the time.

John was keen to compensate me for the embarrassment and asked if I could ride. Sadly, I could not, so I missed the chance of riding to hounds. Then he invited me to an event at the stately home of the Earl of Y……. It was supposed to be a get together of friends with a free feed. At least that was how he sold it to me but it was actually very different.

The house was of the sort that I had usually paid to look round and it was full of people who owned large tracts of land or major corporations. The accents were of the type that Monty Python would have parodied, but they were perfectly normal in that house. The women looked as if they had stepped straight off the cat walk, even if some of them were models of the older age group or the larger size.

The staircase rose from the entrance hall up to a mezzanine and then on upwards almost indefinitely. Sat on the stairs was an elderly man who looked to have belonged in a care home but he had a sparkle in his eye and a clear sense of belonging in this environment. As women passed him, he lifted their dresses with his walking stick and made bawdy comments that seemed to be accepted.

We were approached by a butler in tail coats as soon as we entered and he showed us into a large reception room. There we were offered envelopes of different prices from a silver tray. Some of the envelopes had prices on them that ran into hundreds of pounds. I saw one that cost five pounds and I grabbed it eagerly as it was explained that the price related to the number of raffle tickets in each envelope. The butler looked at me as if I was the local tramp who had gate-crashed the event.

I was then handed a glass of champagne and allowed to wander round the buffet which was spread throughout the room. There was every sort of exotic food which included a huge blue stilton cheese that people helped themselves to by scooping it out of the middle of the cheese. A servant regularly poured port into the cheese which was a whole different way of living to that which I was used to, especially after a year living off operational food during the Miners' Strike.

As the champagne released my inhibitions, I started to enjoy the event. I did not win a prize, though John won a brace of pheasants from the estate, a bottle of brandy and several bottles of wine. He was staggering about, looking unused to his evening dress and as we left, he put a flat cap on his head. He climbed into the drivers' seat of his Range Rover, his wife sat next to him and I joined about six others in the back. He swung the vehicle out of the driveway and onto the main road. For about ten minutes we were travelling about as fast as that type of vehicle would go and then as we passed a side road a blue light was suddenly turned on and a police car was following us.

John was well over the drink drive limit and he immediately pulled up. He grabbed the two pheasants and a bottle of wine. He met the officer half way between the two vehicles and there was a good degree of laughing before the pheasants and wine were handed to the officer. The officer pulled his police car in front of us and then set off steadily. John got in and followed.

"We've got an escort," said John. "'I've told him that I'm giving the Chief Constable a lift home. I also said the present was from the Chief".

We were escorted all the way to John's house where we all got out and waved the officer off on his way. I do not know who else could have carried that off.

Several weeks later he asked me if I would lend him some uniform for a fancy-dress party at his house. I did not want to let him down but I also realized that he often sailed close to the wind. I lent him trousers, a tunic without identification and a helmet with the badge removed. He invited me to his party and there he was resplendent in full uniform with badges that he had bought at a memorabilia shop. As parking became difficult for his guests John slipped out of the house. I thought nothing of it and really enjoyed the night.

The following day one of Johns' neighbours came to the station. He complained that John had been impersonating a police officer. He had gone round the cul de sac writing imitation parking tickets. As a result, many of the local residents had removed their cars from the street before his guests parked there. I told the man that I would look into it and eventually reported that John had got a costume from a fancy-dress shop, I had given him advice about his future behaviour and the neighbour was placated.

A month later I felt that John had gone a step too far. He lived in a fairly remote area. His house was in a small development that overlooked a farm which stretched out below. One day I was called to that farm and the landowner had been shot in the entrance to his barn. There were few murders in this area and clearly there would be massive media attention. We closed the lane to the farm and believed that we had control of the scene of the crime. John rang me to ask what was taking place and, as I knew he could see what was happening from his house, I told him briefly.

Later that day film appeared on the TV news, the newspaper had photographs of the investigating officer at the scene and of people coming and going. Initially I could not work out where the shots were taken from. Some police officers thought that we were the victims of telescopic photography. In the end I went to Johns for a cup of tea and there I walked into his cottage media industry. He had got a TV camera unit set up in his living room, there were reporters, cameramen and two of his workers providing food and drink. The media had a perfect vantage point and John was making a small fortune in providing it!

That soured our relations for some time. He was not wholly trustworthy and was willing to exploit any friendship. Eventually he had an affair with a much younger woman, his wife left him and he lost his garage and his financial backing. His house was empty, except for stacks of empty beer cans which were built up round the fireplace. He remained eccentric though his number of 'friends' declined dramatically.

In an attempt to maintain his lifestyle his behaviour became more and more strange. He still had an old Jaguar with a large sun roof. He acquired a parachute and decided that he would do some paragliding from his car. He and his new partner drove to Lincolnshire and found a long straight road. He climbed out of the sunroof onto the top of the car. As the speed picked up, he released the parachute and with a violent jerk he was thrown into the air. He floated behind the car and steadied into a fairly safe progress. Sadly, all straight roads come to an end. The Jaguar approached a T junction and his partner had to stop to give way to vehicles on the main road. John sailed over the car and over the cars on the main road until he crashed into an advertising hoarding at the other side of the junction. He broke several bones but seemed happy that he had tried it out and added to his legend.

I left that area soon after that escapade and I did not hear from him for some time. I was working in a Headquarters Department when out of the blue I received a phone call. He was about to attend a Masonic dinner in the old part of the city. He told me a story of his victimization by the city police who issued him ticket after ticket. He wanted my help.

I checked the number of tickets that had been issued to him and only three were in the area of the Masonic Hall. Those three had been issued over eighteen months by three different officers for parking on double yellow lines. I told him that he should park where permitted and I told him where those areas were. They were too far from the venue and especially not if it were raining. I never heard from him again.

A few weeks later I heard of his later crazy behaviour. He decided that he would cross the estuary on water skis which would ensure that he arrived near the Masonic Hall without a vehicle. His partner would control the speed boat. He would wear a dry suit over his evening dress. He even told the local newspaper. On the night of the event, he set off crossing the wide expanse of muddy water which was a major shipping channel. To start with it was going well, they were half way across without any incident.

Suddenly John hit a large piece of wood. He hurtled upwards and down before his partner could stop. He had not let go of the drag rope and he hit the water with a massive impact. He was knocked out and was only saved by a miracle. He spent weeks in traction. That was the last incident I ever found out about. I invited him to my wedding and he was coming until the last minute but I have never seen him again. His exciting life gave me a sense of buzz that left a gap in following years.

In the last months that I spent as an operational inspector life took a mundane sort of course. It seemed as if there were no new experiences, just variations of a theme.

CHAPTER EIGHTEEN

A NEW DIRECTION.

One spring day I was about to end my shift and was thinking of a steady jog home in the early sunshine. As I made my way to the locker room to get into my running kit I was approached by a young constable. He said that he was trying to get a lift to a far point of the sub division. He had been told to attend a sudden death and this was to be his first. I remembered mine and decided that I would take him and help with it.

As we drove towards the address, he told me that he was more worried about this than anything else he had been sent to. I told him about my first sudden death and the problems I had had with empathising with the dead.

I was still thinking of that long ago day as we turned into the street that the constable had been sent to. It was a pleasant residential area. The gardens were well looked after and daffodils were in full flower. An elderly lady approached our car as we got out.

"He's around the back. He's dead. I called it in. You've taken your time."

Before I could respond to her the new constable said,
"Well, he's not going anywhere if he's dead. Is he?"

His response was abrasive and callous, particularly if this was the wife of the deceased. However, I must admit that I had similar thoughts.

"How did you find him?" I asked the lady.

"I heard a rumbling noise and I came round from next door. He's round the back it gave me quite a shock."

We walked round the back of the house that the lady had pointed out and there we saw a sight that we were not prepared for. The man was almost erect and his feet were just touching the floor. He was held in that position by a plastic-coated washing line that came from the upper floor of the house and led to a noose round his neck. The man, about fifty years old, had clearly hung himself. He had wrapped the line round a bed and put a noose round his neck he had then jumped from the upstairs window.

What mental state the man must have been in I could not even contemplate. He had not made a good job of killing himself. The weight of his body had dragged the bed across the floor and nearer the window. Also, the line had had elastic properties and it had stretched. His fall had not broken his neck and he must have died by a slow and painful strangulation. The line had dug into his neck, his eyes were shut and his skin was cold.

I got a knife from the kitchen and told the constable to hold the man while I cut the line above the knot of the noose. As we did this the man's eyes opened, he made a croaking noise and suddenly grabbed the constable. The young officer panicked and let go, just as I cut through the line, and the man fell to the floor. He was, however, very clearly alive. I quickly cut the noose which would not loosen off and we called an ambulance.

After he was taken to hospital, we checked the house and found a suicide note and a pile of bank statements. The cause was clear, the despair was evident. I wondered whether we were too late or too early for him. There was certainly no happy ending, he survived for over a day but did not regain consciousness. The constable did not receive an easy introduction to sudden death and, like me, perhaps learned more about himself than procedure.

The mental state that people get themselves into prior to a suicide attempt is almost unimaginable. I remember one occasion when a young man had attempted suicide. Having survived, he agreed to his parents' suggestion that he sought treatment. He voluntarily admitted himself to a mental hospital. For a time, he seemed to be coming to terms with life and was looking better. Then one day he climbed out of the dormitory window and ran away.

Only hours later he jumped off a high bridge over a turbulent river. By a miracle he jumped off at the precise moment a canoeist came under the bridge. The canoeist dragged the comatose body (knocked out when he hit the water) and telephoned the police. We arrived and took him straight back to the hospital. Later the same day as the light faded and a thick mist settled over the area the man escaped again. This time he returned to the bridge and jumped again. There was no miracle. The young man jumped from the wrong place and plummeted into the concrete support of the bridge. What a total waste of life.

To most people there is nothing amusing about death, yet the Police use 'Black Humour' as a way of dealing with fatality. I once visited a colleague who had crashed his motorcycle on his way home. He was in traction with almost every large bone in his body broken. He had taken a turn straight into a car which was on the wrong side of the road. A second or so later a taxi full of surgeons from the City Hospital came upon the accident scene on their way home from a dinner. If they had not been there my colleague would have died. They kept him alive until the ambulance arrived.

The motorcycle could have been brushed up, there were no metal parts that resembled anything that was once a motor vehicle.

When I arrived at the Hospital my colleague lay there unable to move and with his head and neck in a 'halo' (a device for setting broken necks) There were other officers in his bedroom and we sat round his bed, no one spoke, he looked like he was hanging to life by a thread. Then a big, burly, red-faced traffic officer came into the room and said,

"If you get paid out, can I have the back tyre form your bike?"

For a moment the room remained silent and then the patient smiled. Everyone else laughed. The back tyre would have been all that was left, the situation was horrendous yet the comment had broken the ice.

A sergeant I worked with did once share his embarrassing moment with me. His was certainly more dramatic than mine and it seriously set his career back. He had long wished to work as a Coroner's Officer. I could not understand anyone wanting to do that job, but I suppose it takes all sorts!

Having mentioned his desire to fulfil the role at a number of annual appraisals he was finally given the opportunity to stand in during the temporary absence of the usual Coroner's Officer. For several weeks he enjoyed every minute of it. He even began keeping his lunch box in the freezer with the bodies, just to show that he was feeling at home in the job.

On one occasion an old lady who had died in a nursing home was brought into the mortuary. The Coroner's Officer had to complete a form prior to the release of the body to the funeral directors. The sergeant was supposed to do checks on the lady's medical history as she had not seen a doctor for years. He did not do the checks, he cut corners and ticked boxes on the form in a way that would speed up procedures. One of the boxes he ticked indicated that the lady was not fitted with a pacemaker device.

The body was released and on the day of the lady's cremation there was a massive bang from the burning unit as the deceased's pacemaker exploded. The door to the incinerator had been blown off and considerable damage was done. I am pretty certain there would have been no ashes to give to the deceased's' relatives.

The sergeant was removed from the post immediately and he spent the rest of his career telling people he had been unlucky to have encountered the type of pacemaker the old lady had been fitted with. His story was that the device was based on a vacuum. Whether he was unlucky or not I would have kept the whole thing quiet.

I had been a uniform, operational inspector for two years. I was happy, content and felt able to deal with any challenge that the passing days threw up. I had not been to the Force Headquarters in those years, I had not seen a Chief Officer and I had lost contact with the officers I had previously worked with. When I thought about it, I seemed to have dropped off the radar. No one was planning anything for me. I could carry on where I was, possibly for years, until I no longer wanted to move. A whole new set of Chief Officers would arrive and focused on their own upwardly mobile careers; they would know nothing of me.

My steady drift from shift to shift was suddenly disrupted when I was sent on a course for newly promoted inspectors. I did not think of myself as newly promoted; however, I had missed out during the months of the Miners' Strike. It was two weeks in another Force and so I looked forward to it as a change with no working night shifts for a while. Part of the course involved completing a Diploma in Business Studies which was interesting.

I remember very little of what went on in the classrooms, other than I found myself to be very poor at public speaking. What I do remember was almost getting dragged in to a major disciplinary investigation. That investigation resulted in several officers being sacked. I became involved purely by being in the wrong place at the wrong time.

There was a pub near the training college which had a certain disreputable fame across Yorkshire. The barmaids all had good figures, they wore hot pants and when not serving beer they played tambourines while standing on the top of the bar. As the nights got going some of the barmaids were topless and anything seemed to go. At the time it seemed to be the place to be, though now I can remember my shoes sticking to the carpet and the beer being almost tasteless and very gassy.

There were several courses running at the training centre, though the majority of the students were attending a junior detective course. Those on the CID course worked hard, they had to in order to pass, but they consumed beer like there was no tomorrow. Some of them only arrived back at the centre an hour or two before lessons started. There were always parties being held in the students' rooms in the accommodation block and people often woke up wondering which room they were in.

One night I went out with two fellow students from the inspectors' course. They lived locally and they dropped me off not far from the centre as they were living at home. I had a pint as I walked up the road where they had left me. I thought about getting a meal but found the Indian take away to be closed. It was lit up and there were staff but the door was locked.

As I entered the training centre accommodation, I was invited to a party in one of the female detectives' rooms. Technically this would constitute an offence as there was a strict policy of segregating men and women. As you entered the part of the building that women lived in there was a sign with a large red hand and the logo "NO MEN BEYOND THIS POINT". I was not the only man at the party and it was amazing how many could pack into one single study room.

Just as I was about to leave, a group of five or six male detectives arrived in a very agitated state. Something or someone had upset them and I did hear the word 'Packy' used several times. As I went down the stairs a little later the same group rushed past me. Some had what looked like shoe polish on their faces and others wore hoods and woolly hats. They clearly were on a mission and almost running as they left the building.

I did not find out what happened until I was told the following morning. The detectives had been making their way back when they also decided to get a curry, at the very take away I had attempted to enter. The staff were praying as it was Ramadan and they did not open up as the officers banged on the door. When they were ignored, the students became abusive and eventually provoked a reaction from the staff who poured out of the takeaway. Realising they were outnumbered the detectives ran for the safety of the training centre and were pursued all the way by angry Asians.

I had seen the young men when they came into the accommodation block and I also saw them leave. Though I did not know it at the time they were intent on securing revenge for their perceived humiliation. They hurled abuse at the staff in the takeaway and eventually threw a large paving stone through the window of the targeted building. Again, they were chased off and it must have been obvious to the staff that they were dealing with police officers.

I was updated on what had happened as I sat eating my breakfast and the canteen went quiet as the names of those who had been involved were called to attend the office of a

Detective Superintendent. To my amazement and shock my name was called out at the same time as theirs.

I was kept waiting in a corridor for over an hour before being called into a smoke-filled room. The superintendent was red faced, with salt and pepper hair and he smelled of a strong after shave.

"I understand you were involved in the attack on the Asian takeaway last night?"

It was easy to reply that I had nothing to do with it.

"You were seen by students to leave with those on the detectives course. A member of staff at the takeaway says you were there just before their first visit.?"

This was not looking good. I told my interrogator that I did not know those involved. I had only found out what had happened that morning. I did say that I had intended to get a curry but the door was closed.

"So why were you leaving at the same time they did?"

I said I was going to bed. I had been out with two inspectors and they would tell him what time they had dropped me off.

"So why were you in the wrong part of the accommodation block at the same time as them and contrary to the rules of the centre.?"

I had to admit that I had been to the party. I had seen those who left, but I did not leave the building.

The superintendent sat there for a while looking at his pen. Then he looked at me for a long time.

"You could be sent home to your Force if you have broken the rules. If you give me a full statement of what you saw then we will overlook your misdemeanour. You should leave policewomen alone; they are hot and they are as much trouble as police property and paperwork. Get out and have a good day"

Yet again I had drifted into trouble without really doing anything. I did give a statement, but it could have served as little more than providing continuity in the case against the officers. Some were sacked and all were sent back to their Forces. As far as I know my actions were never brought to the attention of my senior officers.

Some officers seem to live a charmed life when they break the rules. Others, like me, seemed to attract trouble like a magnet. I remember one officer who joined the Police on leaving the Army. He was a popular young man but he had little sense of discipline or even sense. In a rugby match against an army unit, he said he was going to knock out their officer and he did. He was once having an affair with a woman who worked as an 'Avon Lady' (selling cosmetics and scents from home) and on one night he left his watch on the bedside table at her house. His wife had asked where his watch was and he obviously had to get it back.

The following day he was taking part in an athletics track meeting in South Yorkshire. The sergeant in charge of the athletics section had struggled to get a van as the Miners' Strike was in full swing. The sergeant promised to get the van back early. After the event, everyone returned to the van to go home. The constable was sat in the driving seat and had locked himself in the front which was separated from the seating area by a metal grille. He refused to let anyone get in the front with him. He then drove the vehicle, with the team in it, on a round trip of sixty miles to get his watch. We were well over due to return the vehicle and theoretically the constable had taken the vehicle without consent. The sergeant decided that he had allowed his authority to be overridden and obviously felt he would suffer as much as the constable so he never reported it.

On another occasion the same officer had attended a fight in a fish and chip shop. He no doubt punished the fighters by applying his own very physical techniques. Two had to be taken to hospital and a very smartly dressed man, who had not been involved in the trouble, took an objection to the officers' methods. The man informed the officer that he knew the Chief Constable and he would report the officer. There was a pause and then the officer grabbed the man's hand and pulled an expensive diamond ring off one of his fingers. Without pause he threw the ring in the Fish Fryer,

"Tell him about that then!" Said the officer.

He survived that incident and several others before he was found driving a marked police vehicle with his dog and a shotgun on private property. For that he was posted to another division where he should have kept his head down. Sadly, he did not. He was called to a secondary school where some money had been taken from the tea fund tin in the teacher's common room. The constable asked if any pupils were thought to have been responsible and no information was forthcoming; so, he radioed for two vans to be sent to the school. He then arrested every member of staff and ended the days teaching.

There had been no evidence against anyone. I suspect he was just having a bad day and he often said he did not like people who thought they were better than he was. He could be effective at times but he was in the wrong job at the wrong time, though he later became a member of the Police Federation (the Police Officers 'Union') where he was able to help other officers from his own experience with discipline matters. In one sense it is amazing that he survived and retired with a pension, but he had a physical presence which made many officers feel safe when they were working with him. He was a genuinely nice bloke but would not survive five minutes in today's politically correct world.

Another constable was a dedicated police officer who worked hard and had never once been in disciplinary trouble. Then one day he arrested a young girl for being drunk and disorderly, she was found to have a small quantity of cannabis in her possession. In the Charge Office he obviously had an immense empathy with the girl. When she was released, he took her home in his own car and I believe there was a brief relationship. The girl was subsequently arrested again and when she was not so well treated the second time, she told the sergeant that the first officer had given her cannabis back to her. The officer had secreted an offence and also supplied drugs. He was gone from the Force within hours and became persona non grata from then onwards.

I was also present on one occasion when a sergeant must have seen his career flash before his eyes. I had visited the Charge Office to check some papers and I was sat at the desk when a prisoner was brought in. A tall, strange looking lady stood between two male officers. She was wearing a green tweedy jacket and matching skirt and she had a large pair of brown brogues on her feet.

The 'lady' had been arrested following a disturbance at the WRVS Office.

"What is your name?" Asked the sergeant.

"I am Lady Astor of the Manor." Came the reply in a strange high-pitched voice.

"Right, I am not messing around with you. Search her Matron." The sergeant said, addressing the civilian Matron who was there to deal with female prisoners. The initial search proceeded and after a short time the Matron began to check the pockets in the skirt. Then suddenly the Matron stepped back, obviously shocked.

"You dirty bastard. This isn't a woman; it's got a cock."

The sergeant, who was very protective of his staff, leaned forward across the Charge Room desk and grabbed the prisoner by the front of her blouse. He pulled her towards him and as he did so the prisoner screamed and collapsed onto the floor. The Matron knelt beside the prostrate figure and began to loosen her clothing. It soon became obvious that the prisoner was bleeding.

By now the sergeant was also in a state of shock and stood there speechless. I rang the Police Doctor on call and the Matron began to check for the source of the prisoners bleeding. The first injury seemed to be that both nipples were torn and bleeding. It appeared that the nipples had been pierced and the rings that had been in them had been dragged out when the sergeant grabbed 'her' blouse.

The arrival of the doctor revealed the full extent of the injuries. The prisoner had had both nipples, 'her' belly button and the foreskin of 'her' penis pierced. All the sites were connected by a chain that held the penis in an upwards position. The sergeants tug had pulled the rings out of each site and the most difficult to stop bleeding was the penis injury. An ambulance conveyed the prisoner to the hospital.

Those who had been present when the prisoner arrived could not believe what they had just seen. The sergeant still seemed to be in shock while the Matron was clearly enjoying the notoriety that her involvement had brought.

I know that the sergeant kept his job, there was no complaint of assault and it may be that the prisoner was too embarrassed having been found out. I also believe that the injured party had mental health issues and never again came to police attention.

In my later career I witnessed numerous strange outcomes to disciplinary issues but the telling of those must wait for another day. After the inspectors' course I was called to see the Divisional Commander. It was a strange meeting. He told me how highly he rated me as an operational inspector but then out of the blue he said I should transfer to a Headquarters post. He did not have one in mind and he did not know if there were any posts vacant. The upshot of this meeting was that he felt things had become too easy for me and I needed a challenge.

I have come to realise that the Divisional Commander was right. People can disappear in a Police Force. I know of at least two who fall into that category. The first was an inspector seconded to the Home Office for two years. He was still there after eight years, there was no paperwork formalizing any extensions and no one ever asked for him back. One officer, however, managed to disappear without even leaving our Force.! That individual worked as a Traffic Police Officer until he hurt his wrist in an accident whilst on duty. While recuperating before his return to full duties he was posted to the Headquarters Garage Office where he would help administer the repair and servicing of police vehicles. There under the noses of Chief Officers he remained for seven years. He wandered around the garage and storeroom wearing a brown dustcoat.

Whilst he was there the supervisors and managers in the Office gradually changed and he became a fixture and a symbol of continuity. I never knew he was a police officer until one evening we both got on the same train and both got off several stops later where the train terminated. There the officer appeared confused, he smelled of drink and looked a little dishevelled. He explained to me that he had gone to sleep and missed his stop which had been much earlier in the trains' journey. I sat with him while he waited for a train back to his destination and he filled me in with his career and the details of his current employment.

It was obvious that he wished to remain in the Garage Office away from the front line of policing and shift working until his eventual retirement. He managed to remain there for several months after our meeting until a new manager found that he was not on the establishment of the Office. He was by this time totally unsuitable to be deployed as a police officer. He was unfit, untrained and he had not even driven a car for several years. He was posted to an Enquiry Office until his retirement came along. By that date he had spent thirty percent of his entire career not involved in police duties.

Whereas the missing officers may have dodged out of front-line service delivery, there were some who did not do a lot when they were there and in uniform. I once asked an officer for a report on an incident he had witnessed and when it arrived it was neatly typed but the signature stated BOBBY SLATER and was printed in block capitals and written in pencil. I thought that a typist had written the name for the officer to sign there after she had typed it. I sent the report to the officers' sergeant to get the report signed properly.

The reality was stranger than fiction. Some years previously the officer had been personally recruited by the Chief Constable of the then Borough Police Force that then operated from our station. He was one of a number of Scottish League football players who were recruited towards the end of their professional football careers. The Chief Constable wanted his Force Football Team to be the best in the area and football skills were high on the list of those required by new officers.

So highly were those skills regarded that no one had bothered to ask Robert Slater, left winger, if he could read and write! In 1985 he had still not mastered writing and the Force which had recruited him no longer existed. PC Slater recorded everything he wanted to say on a cassette and the typists did the rest on his forms, statements and reports. He was quite well thought of at the station, he was always polite and while he did very little his paperwork was always extremely neat.... produced as it was by professional typists.

So, you can see why I would begin to feel overlooked in my 'sleepy hollow' and why the Divisional Commander might just have it right.

After that meeting I started to look at posts that were advertised in a document called 'Force Orders'. That publication came out every week, it updated officers on legislation and procedural changes, it listed promotions, postings, retirements and disciplinary action outcomes. Having scanned them for about a month I found a vacancy listed for an inspector in the Force Research and Support Department. I had no idea what that would involve but I applied for it. My fellow inspectors seemed shocked that I would want to get involved with that. A detective Inspector took me to one side in the bar and gave me the following advice.

"You will regret it if you leave here. Headquarters is a cess pit of back stabbers and idlers. Keep out of there would be my advice"

I did not take that advice. In the years that followed I often think back on that advice. There was a lot of truth in it. Perhaps life would be boring if you always took good advice. I did get that job and it was an immense turning point in my life. Perhaps I'll tell you about the back stabbers at another time!

As they say "onwards and upwards".

Printed in Great Britain
by Amazon